TORAH
AND
FLORA

Louis I. Rabinowitz

NEW YORK

Published by
SANHEDRIN PRESS
a division of Hebrew Publishing Company
80 Fifth Avenue, New York, N.Y. 10011

Library of Congress Cataloging in Publication Data

Rabinowitz, Louis Isaac, 1906–
   Torah and flora.

   Includes index.
    1. Bible. O.T. Pentateuch—Addresses, essays, lectures. 2. Bible—Natural history—Addresses, essays, lectures.
I. Title.
BS1225.4.R3   222'.1'06   76–58906
ISBN 0–88482–917–0

CONTENTS

Introduction   v

The Fig   1
The Lesson of the Olive Leaf   3
The Sacred Tree of Shechem   5
The Trees of Hospitality   7
Isaac the Tree Planter   10
The Fragrance of the Field   12
Rashi Nods   14
The Oak which is Another   16
Floral Names   18
Brotherly Plants   21
Improving with Age   23
Fruitful or Fruitless   25
The Burning Bush   27
An Agricultural Calendar   30
Milk and Honey   32
The Desalinating Tree   35
Out of the Ashes   39
Thorns and Thistles   41
The Speech of the Trees   43
Olive Oil   46
Sinner's Spice   52

The Shittah   55
The Pomegranate   61
Lots of Wood . . . and Walnuts!   64
Nothing but the Best   70
Cypress or Song   73
Before Dacron   76
The Rites of Humility   78
Lily Among the Thorns   81
The Sycamore   84
The Humble Barley   87
Abusing the Soil   90
The Forlorn Juniper   93
Nicholas Dates   96
The Nazirite   98
Egyptian Salad   101
A Coincidence of Dates   105
The Rod of Aaron   108
Cedar, King or Commoner   111
A Garden by the Euphrates   114
The Rotem   116
The Desert and the Sown   119
The Caper   122
The Carob   127
Poor, Learned Tree!   133
Honey   136
Provision of Food   139
Trees in Jerusalem   141
Leket, Shikhḥah and Pe'ah   144
Spices   147
Gall and Wormwood   149
Wine of Lebanon   153
Vine of Sodom   155
Fraudulent Flora   158

Indexes
   A. Scriptural References   161
   B. Flora   164

INTRODUCTION

The Flora of the Bible is a fascinating subject, and considerable research has been done on it since the classical three volume *Die Flora Der Juden* by Immanuel Loew.

The present work, which is in essence a selection from the weekly column bearing the same title as this volume, which appeared regularly for over 12 years in the week-end edition of the *Jerusalem Post*, does not claim to be a scientific work adding to the knowledge of Biblical Botany. It represents the fruit of personal observation acquired in the course of my weekly hikes through the lovely countryside of Judea, and in addition reflects the love which the rabbis of the Talmud and Midrash had for the phenomena of Nature and the homiletical use they make of it. There is virtually not a plant or an agricultural product which they do not press into service in this manner, and the material, of which this volume represents only a minor fraction, is almost inexhaustible.

The publication of this volume is in response to the extremely large number of readers all over the world who have asked that the material be made available in the more permanent form of a volume, and it is hoped that it will be a source of pleasure to its readers, adding to their love of the Bible and of the Land of Israel which is its topographical framework.

the fig

BERESHIT. GENESIS 1:1–6:8.

> *And they sewed fig-leaves together, and made them-*
> *selves girdles.*
>   GENESIS 3:7

The fig is the first tree mentioned by name in the Bible, albeit
it is not the tree or the fruit which is referred to, but its wide
leaves with which Adam and Eve covered their nakedness after
they ate of the fruit of the Forbidden Tree, the Tree of the
Knowledge of Good and Evil. It gains honorable mention in
the Bible in two other contexts; it is one of the Seven Species
which are enumerated in Deuteronomy 8:8 as those agricultural
products which are "the glory of the Land of Israel," and the
halcyon days of universal peace are described as the time when
"they shall sit every man under his vine and under his fig tree,
and none shall make them afraid" (Micah 4:4).

In rabbinic legend, however, the fig appears in a much less
favorable context, which demotes it from the honorable mention
in the Bible. It is characteristic of the rabbis—and a number of
examples will be given in this volume—to fill the lacunae of
the written narrative and dispel the anonymity which shrouds
many of its details. Accordingly they apply themselves to the
question of the identification of this Forbidden Tree, the eating
of whose fruit caused the expulsion of Primal Man from the
Garden of Eden. Various suggestions are put forward, all of them
giving reasons for the choice.

In the Talmud (*Berakhot* 40b) three suggestions are put forth
by various rabbis: wheat (reasons are given for regarding it as
a "tree"), the vine, and the fig. The Midrash, *Genesis Rabbah*
15:8, adds to them the citron (the *etrog*) which is emphatically
approved by Naḥmanides (see his fascinating commentary on
Leviticus 23:40). The fig, however, is most favored, on the

1

grounds that "with that which they sinned they repaired their misdeed," and for this reason it was with leaves of this tree that they covered their nakedness. The Midrash gives a homely parable: "It is the parable of the son of a king who misbehaved with one of the maidservants. When the father heard of the misdeed he drove them from the palace. The homeless prince sought asylum with all the maidservants, but they rejected him. The one with whom he had misbehaved, however, opened her door to him." For this reason, of all the fruit-bearing trees only the timber of the fig tree was used as fuel for the sacrificial altar.

the lesson of the olive leaf

NO'AḤ. GENESIS 6:9–11 END.

And the dove came in to him at eventide, and lo, in her mouth an olive-leaf freshly plucked.

GENESIS 8:11

After the fig comes the olive, and like it, it is only the leaf and not the fruit which is first mentioned. The olive leaf which the dove brought back to Noah in the Ark was the sign to him that the flood waters had substantially subsided.

We shall have ample opportunity to deal with the fruit itself with its invaluable oil (see Olive Oil); this chapter confines itself to the beautiful moral lessons which the rabbis derive from that olive leaf brought back in the beak of the dove. References to "the rabbis" in this volume normally refer to the ancient rabbis of the Talmud and the Midrash, but deriving homiletical and ethical lessons from Scripture is an exercise indulged in by the rabbis throughout the ages, and of the two examples given here, although the first belongs to the former category, the second, no less beautiful, is by a rabbi who lived in the present century. The talmudic homily is based on the verse which is the subject of this chapter. The nominal form of the verb *taraf* which means "torn," and is here rendered "freshly picked," also means "food," and it is this which is the basis of the lovely homily of the rabbis in the Talmud. There was in the choice of the olive, according to them, a silent but eloquent symbol of the passion for freedom on the part of every caged bird—as of every human being. The olive is traditionally the most bitter of plants, the bitterness encompassing the leaf, the twigs and the fruit. And with it the dove indicated to Noah the profound and moving message, "Better the food which comes from the Holy One blessed be He, even though it be bitter, than the most succulent of dainties if one is dependent on man for it."

3

The modern homily occurs in a recently published volume of talmudic glosses, *Gilyonei Yo'el* (1970), by the late Rabbi Joel Herzog, father of the late Chief Rabbi Herzog. The author quotes an equally beautiful homily in the name of Rabbi Joseph Sherashevsky of Slonim. The sin which brought about the Flood was unbridled promiscuity. The Talmud (*Sanhedrin* 108a) explains the verse, "For all flesh had corrupted its way upon the earth" (Genesis 6:12)—"Beasts and animals copulated indiscriminately with one another as they did with men." According to the Talmud, however, in the worlds both of flora and fauna there is one outstanding example of chastity and lack of promiscuity. In the animal world it is the dove, of which the Talmud states, "If the Torah had not been given to us we should have learned the virtue of chastity from the dove" (*Eruvin* 100b). In the world of flora it is stated that hybrid plants can be produced from the grafting of all trees except the olive (Jerusalem Talmud, *Kilaim* 1:7). And the combination of this paragon of chastity among birds and the unique example of lack of promiscuity among trees was to bring to Noah the heartening message that not only the flood had subsided, but also that perversion of nature which had brought it about.

Thus does the "olive branch" in Jewish tradition convey more than the ideal of peace; it teaches the lessons of the virtue of liberty and the restraint of the unbridled lusts of man.

the sacred tree of shechem

LEKH LEKHA. GENESIS 12–17.

> *And Abram passed through the land unto the place*
> *of Shechem, unto* eilon moreh . . . GENESIS 12:6

When Abraham (Abram), in accordance with the Divine
command, reached the Land of Canaan, he eventually came to
eilon moreh. Rashi, following the Targum, the Aramaic translation
of the Torah, denies that *eilon*—unlike *elah*, the pistacia, and *allon*,
the oak—is a tree, and maintains that it means a plain, a rendering
which is adopted by the Authorized Version of the Bible. Most
commentators, however, regard it as referring to a tree, and
the Revised Version, as well as those of the Jewish Publication
Society and the New English Bible, render the word *eilon* as
"terebinth." But what about the other word, *moreh*? It is obvious
from the scriptural passage that the *eilon* of *moreh* was a significant
landmark even before the advent of Abraham, and that its
significance belongs to the idolatrous pre-patriarchal Canaanite
era. The word *moreh* means "one who teaches" or "gives instruction" and the reasonable suggestion has been put forward
that in this context it means "an oracle," a sacred tree which was
used for divination and soothsaying (W.R. Smith, *Lectures on
the Religion of the Semites* (1889–94), 193ff.).

The *eilonei moreh* are mentioned again, in the plural, in
Deuteronomy 11:30, but in addition we are told that when Jacob
escaped from Shechem after the massacre of the inhabitants by
his sons Simeon and Levi, he hid the idols which he had taken
from members of his household "under the *elah* which was by
Shechem" (Genesis 35:4). That passage is the basis of an incident
related in the Midrash, which reflects the bitter enmity which
existed at that time between the Samaritans whose holy place is
Mount Gerizim, and the Jews whose spiritual center is, of course,

Jerusalem. Rabbi Ishmael ben Joseph of Galilee was making a pilgrimage to Jerusalem. When he reached Shechem he met a Samaritan whom he informed that he was on his way to worship on the Temple Mount. The conversation took place at a certain tree, called there a *platanus* (usually a plane tree, but in a fragment of the translation of the Bible into Greek by the third-century proselyte Symmachus it is given as the translation of *elah*), and the Samaritan said to him, "Is it not better to pray on this holy mountain than on the accursed one in Jerusalem?" Incensed at this insulting reference to the Temple Mount, Ishmael answered him with equal rudeness, "You are like a dog which digs for a buried carcass. It is because you know that an idol is buried under this tree that you regard it as sacred, as it is written 'and Jacob hid the idols under the *elah* which is in Shechem.'" It is not the only reference in the rabbinic literature of the existence of a sacred tree on Mount Gerizim, and it points to the fact that for close to 2,000 years there stood upon that mountain "which is by Shechem" a grove or a tree which was continuously regarded by the non-Jews as sacred.

the trees of hospitality

VA-YERA. GENESIS 18–22.

> . . . *And he stood by them under the tree and they did eat.*　　　　　　　　　　　　　　　GENESIS 18:8
>
> *Abraham planted an* eshel *in Beersheba and called there on the name of the Lord, the Everlasting God.*
> 　　　　　　　　　　　　　　　GENESIS 21:33

Trees of Abraham are mentioned twice in this week's portion. The first is not identified although it is stated that he was sitting under the *eilonei Mamre* when he espied the strangers. It is the tree under which Abraham dispensed hospitality to the three angels disguised as footsore, weary travelers (18:8). The other may be anonymous and may not (21:33). Some authorities regard the word *eshel* in the second verse as referring to a specific tree which is identified with the tamarisk, but others see in the word a grove of trees, and so the Jewish Publication Society version renders it.

In the former verse, even according to the plain meaning, there is justification for the rabbinic typology of Abraham as the prototype and the paragon of hospitality, and every reference to it is lovingly embellished and extended by the rabbis. It is upon the second verse, however, where there is no reference whatsoever to the exercise of this virtue, that the rabbis dwell in order to emphasize this salient virtue of the patriarch. "Resh Lakish said, it teaches us that Abraham made an orchard and planted in it all kinds of choice fruits. Rabbi Judah and Rabbi Nehemiah differed. One said that it was an orchard, the other maintained that it was a hospice" (*Sotah* 10a). In the Midrash (*Genesis Rabbah* 54:8) there is a similar difference of opinion between Rabbi Judah and Rabbi Naḥman. Both transpose the letters of "*eshel*" into "*sha'al*" (to request), and say that it suggests

7

that Abraham said to his guests, "Do not hesitate to ask whatever you may want." But whereas Rabbi Judah confines the request to "figs, dates or pomegranates," Rabbi Naḥman said, "It was a hospice and they could request bread, meat, wine or eggs."

Another interpretation, the best known, makes the word the initial letters of *"akhillah, shetiyyah, leviyyah"*—"food, drink, and escorting on the way." (The frequently quoted *"linah,"* sleeping, for the last letter, which would extend the hospitality from "board" to "lodging" does not occur in the ancient sources.) Still another Midrash maintains that this hospice had entries on all four sides so as to obviate the need for the wayfarers to circumvent the house.

Thus in every possible way the *eshel* is made the supreme example of the lovely virtue of *hakhnasat orḥim*, hospitality to wayfarers, but what is the connection between this first half of the verse and the second half, "And he called there on the name of the Lord, the everlasting God"? Explains the Talmud in the above-mentioned passage, "For *Va-Yikra* [and he called] read *va-yakri* [and he caused to call]." There was a purpose in his hospitality. After his guests had eaten their fill and were ready to arise replete from the table, they naturally thanked their host for his hospitality. But he said unto them, "Is it then of mine that you have partaken? It is of that which belongs to the Lord of the Universe that you have eaten. It is not me whom you should thank and praise. Thank and praise and bless Him Who spoke and the world came into being." And in this way Abraham was instrumental in making his guests "call upon the name of the Lord," and thus he instituted the Grace after Meals.

In 1866 there appeared *The Land and the Book: Thirty years a missionary in Syria and Palestine* by W. M. Thomson, a volume which still makes fascinating reading. Writing of the magnificent oaks that he saw during his visit to the Golan, he comments, "I do not believe that Abraham's celebrated tree at Hebron was a terebinth, as many now affirm without qualification. It is *now* a very *venerable oak* [author's italics], and I saw no terebinth in the neighborhood."

In his actual description of Hebron he states, "Here we are

at the famous oak, and a moment's inspection will show to anyone acquainted with such matters that it can have no connection with Abraham, nor indeed with anyone else who lived more than 1,000 years ago . . . It is a fine old baluta [evergreen oak], however, 25 feet in girth at the ground, and its thick branches extend over an area of 93 feet in diameter. Some 6 feet from the ground the tree forks into three great arms, which again divide as they ascend into innumerable limbs. The location is beautiful, near the head of wadi Sebta, and about two miles north west of this city, and many a picnic is achieved by the Jews of Hebron upon the soft sward that is allowed to grow beneath this noble oak of their Father Abraham.''

This, of course, refers to the first tree, under which the travelers sat while Abraham dispensed hospitality to them. The *eshel* upon which the rabbis base their homily on his hospitability, was in Beersheba.

The century which has passed since Thomson wrote this has dealt harshly with this tree. It is now moribund, shored up and supported like a tottering old man who can no longer stand on his own legs. It is looked after by the neighboring Russian monastery, and is surrounded by a protective fence with a suitable inscription. Steps have now been taken to prolong the life of this tree but its days seem numbered. Next to it, however, stand some of its descendants, growing luxuriantly. It calls to mind the beautiful passage in Job (14:7-9), "For there is hope of a tree; if it be cut down it will sprout again . . . though the root thereof wax old in the earth, and the stock thereof die in the ground, yet through the scent of water it will bud, and bring forth boughs like a plant." And the Midrash actually applies this verse to Abraham and his descendants.

ísaac the tree planter

ḤAYYEI SARAH. GENESIS 23:1–25:18.

> *And Isaac went out* la-su'aḥ *in the field at eventide, and he lifted up his eyes and, behold, there were camels coming.*
> GENESIS 24:63

The word *si'aḥ* in Hebrew has two distinct and different meanings. It means "a bush" (cf. 21:15) and it means "speech." This double meaning is the basis of a Midrash on Genesis 2:5. The literal meaning of the phrase is "and every plant [*si'aḥ*] of the field." But the Midrash, basing itself upon the alternative meaning of the word, makes the beautiful comment: "It seemed as though all the trees were holding converse with one another" or "it seemed that all the trees were whispering to all creation."

It is a similar alternative meaning of the word which, according to two medieval rationalist biblical commentators, makes Isaac the first recorded fruit farmer in the Bible. The verse under discussion in this chapter tells us of the first meeting of Isaac with his chosen bride, Rebekah, chosen by the faithful servant of his father Abraham at his master's bidding. The word *la-su'aḥ* is the verbal form of *si'aḥ*, and accordingly not only does the English Bible render it "to meditate," but the Talmud also translates it as "to pray" and since it was "towards evening" the rabbis derive from the verse the proof that Isaac instituted the afternoon prayer.

Ibn Ezra, however, connects the word with its other meaning and explains that it means that "he was walking among the *siḥim*, the bushes." However, Samuel ben Meir (Rashbam), the grandson of Rashi and a decidedly rationalistic commentator, is much more expansive. The verse previous to the one we are discussing states that Isaac had just come from Beer-Laḥai-Roi "for he dwelt in the Negev." Explains Rashbam: "He had just arrived from the south that day, and went to see how his laborers, who had been engaged in planting gardens and orchards, were carrying out their work. He therefore went out *la-su'aḥ* in the field, i.e., to plant trees and oversee the work of the laborers."

If that attractive explanation could be accepted, it would constitute an interesting stage in the record of the gradual transformation of the Patriarchs from nomadic shepherds to husbandmen. Abraham was essentially a nomad, and subsequently he planted a grove of trees in Beersheba (Genesis 21:23), the first stage towards the settled life of the farmer. Later we read of Isaac sowing grain, and reaping a bountiful harvest (26:12). The interpretation making Isaac the planter of orchards, though chronologically it precedes that of 26:12, takes us a stage further.

But alas, the interpretation is almost disdainfully swept aside by the 19th century Italian Jewish scholar, Samuel David Luzzatto. Commenting on Ibn Ezra's interpretation, he points out laconically that though the noun *si'aḥ* is indeed susceptible of two meanings, both "bush" and "speech," in its verbal form it is found only with the latter meaning, and Isaac emerges only as a man of prayer instead of a pioneer fruit farmer.

the fragrance of the field

TOLEDOT. GENESIS 25:19–28:9.

> *And he came near, and kissed him, and he smelt the smell of his raiment, and he blessed him and said, 'See the smell of my son is as the smell of the field which the Lord hath blessed.'* GENESIS 27:27

We read in this week's portion of the deception practiced by Jacob, at the instigation of his mother Rebekah, on his blind father, Isaac, in order to receive his blessing. Rebekah took the hide of the two goats which she had slaughtered in order to make the "savory meat" and placed them "on the hands and on the smooth of his neck," thus making Jacob seem hairy like Esau. And when Jacob entered his father's presence, we read that he "smelt the smell of his raiment, and he blessed him."

Rabbi Johanan, in the Midrash, makes an apt comment on this verse. He protests, "Is there a more repulsive odor than that of goatskins? And yet Scripture declares, 'See the smell of my son is as the smell of the field which the Lord hath blessed.'" It is fascinating to consider the various answers which are given by different authorities, ancient and medieval, to resolve this difficulty. The Midrash answers that with Jacob there entered the fragrant odor of the Garden of Eden, an explanation which is the starting point for the mystic doctrine of the "Ḥakal Tappuḥin," the celestial "Apple Orchard" of the Kabbalah. The Talmud gives a more mundane explanation. It was the odor of an apple orchard, and apparently in ancient times the apple gave off a much more fragrant smell than it does today (Song of Songs, 7:9).

The rationalistic commentator Ibn Ezra does not confine himself to the apple, nor indeed to the fragrance of the fruit, but to the much more heady fragrance of the blossom. Jacob's

clothes were impregnated with the sweet smell of the blossoming trees, and on this assumption Ibn Ezra actually goes as far
as to suggest that the incident took place during the month
of Nisan when the trees are in the full glory of their blossom. And
in fact, although Ibn Ezra does not mention it, the Talmud
presents in this connection the special blessing which a person
has to say when "he goes out in the month of Nisan and sees the
trees in full bloom."

One of the supercommentaries on Ibn Ezra finds talmudic
support for this establishing of the time of the year, since the
Talmud states that the two goats symbolize the two sacrifices
which were brought on the Festival of Passover: the Paschal
lamb and the ordinary festive offering.

rashi nods

> *And Jacob took him rods of fresh poplar, and of the*
> *almond and of the plane-tree.* GENESIS 30:37

Rashi is the prince of rabbinical commentators but even as Homer can nod, so can Rashi be mistaken!

The Authorized Version translation of Genesis 30:37 is: "And Jacob took him rods of green poplar, and of the hazel and the chestnut tree." Of the three trees thus translated only the first may be correct. The other two are certainly not, and the version in the Jewish Publication Society Bible, "poplar, almond and plane," is almost certainly correct.

The wrong identification is largely due to Rashi. Making the common mistake of identifying trees and plants in the Bible with those which grew in his own country, and disregarding (or being unaware of) the fact that neither the hazel nor the chestnut is indigenous to the Middle East, he identifies the *luz* with the hazel (*kordli*, Latin *Corylus*) and the *armon* with the chestnut (*kastinier*). In the same way he actually identifies the *avati'aḥ* in Numbers 11:5, which is undoubtedly the melon, with—the beetroot!

The Tosafists, the founders of which school were Rashi's own grandsons, point out that the chestnut does not conform to the description given to it in the Talmud, and there is no doubt that the *armon* of the Bible is the plane tree. Modern Hebrew, however, has found a pretty way to give Rashi the respect which is due to him, even if it perpetuates an error: the Aramaic for *armon* is *dulva* and modern Hebrew employs the Hebrew form *dolev* for the plane tree, while retaining *armon* for the chestnut.

Much more surprising, however, is Rashi's identification of the *luz* with the hazel. Ibn Ezra quotes Sa'adiah Gaon (10th century) that the *luz* is none other than the *shaked*, the almond, since it is so called in Arabic, and Hebrew and Arabic and Aramaic are cognate languages.

Both Rashi and Ibn Ezra, however, appear to have overlooked the fact that this identification is already given in the earlier rabbinical literature: in both Talmuds, in the Midrash, and in the Targum. The printed editions of the Midrash explain the "*botnim* and *shekedim*" which Jacob sent to the Prince of Egypt who, unbeknown to him, was his own son, as "oil of *botnim* and oil of *shekedim*"; the *Arukh*, however, has the reading, "oil of *botnim* and oil of *luz*." There is some doubt whether Rashi's undoubted acquaintance with the *Arukh* was a firsthand one, but this reading is already confirmed by the Jerusalem Talmud in dealing with the same subject. Similarly the curious passage of the Babylonian Talmud (*Bekhorot* 8a) which compares the period of gestation of various animals with the period between the blossoming and ripening of the fruit of various trees, equates the 21 days of the hatching of an egg with the 21 days of the blossoming of a *luz*. In *Ecclesiastes Rabbah*, however, on the verse "And the *shaked* shall flourish" (12:5), the Midrash says: "From the blossoming of the almond tree until it yields its fruit is only 21 days, corresponding to the 21 days between the 17th of Tammuz and Tishah be-Av," and the corresponding passage of the Jerusalem Talmud, based on Jeremiah 1:11, "I see a branch of the *shaked*," comments: "Just as the *luz* takes 21 days etc." In short, the identification can be taken as certain. The almond is called both *shaked* and *luz* in Hebrew.

the oak which is another

VA-YISHLAḤ. GENESIS 32:4–36 END.

And Deborah, Rebekah's nurse, died and she was buried below Beth-El under the oak; and the name of it was called allon bakhut [*the oak of weeping*].

GENESIS 35:8

The verse from the portion of this week which will be discussed is certainly puzzling. It comes as an interpolation in the sequence of the narrative: it records an event which appears to be of the most minor importance. What was the nurse of Rebekah, Jacob's mother, doing in the camp of Jacob on his return from his 20 years' enforced exile in Padan Aram? Why should her death be recorded? Why the especial mourning which gives a distinctive name to the oak tree under which she was buried?

The answers to these questions provide an excellent example of the fertile imagination of the rabbis and their capacity to weave a fascinating story out of the most unpromising and vague details.

The first, and only other, time that we hear of the nurse of Rebekah—and she is anonymous there—is some 50 years earlier, or even more if the view of the rabbis that Rebekah was three years old (!) when she was chosen as the bride for Isaac can be accepted. We are told in that connection that when she consented to go to the Land of Israel to become Isaac's wife, "they sent away Rebekah, their sister, and her nurse" (Genesis 24:59). We have to imagine this faithful nurse remaining with her beloved mistress through all those years. But what was she doing in the camp of the son of her mistress? The rabbis explain that when Rebekah urged Jacob to flee to her brother to escape the murderous wrath of Esau, she promised him that as soon as she was sure that Esau's anger had subsided "then I will send and fetch you from there" (27:45). Rebekah chose her now aged and faithful nurse to convey that glad message. Thus it was that she came to be in Jacob's entourage, but the strain of the journey was too much for her and she died shortly after.

Nevertheless, the mourning which gave the tree under which she was buried the name "the Oak of Weeping" was not really for Deborah. Rabbi Samuel ben Naḥman in the Midrash maintains that the word *allon* here does not mean an oak, but is actually the Greek word *allon* which means "another." According to him the verse means "and he buried her instead of another and the name of it was called 'weeping for another'." And who was that "another"? It was none other than his mother Rebekah. Before he had finished mourning for the devoted servant, the news reached him of the death of his mother, and the weeping which was ostensibly for the servant was, in fact, for "another," his mother.

The *Midrash Rabbah* does not trouble to explain the astonishing fact that where the Bible records the death of the servant it passes over the death of the mother in silence. The *Tanḥuma* fills in the lacuna. "They passed over her death in silence that people should not say, 'cursed the womb that had given birth to Esau.'"

And according to another Midrash, that tree was not an oak but a date palm, and the name of the faithful nurse of Rebekah is perpetuated in one other passage in the Bible. There are two Deborahs mentioned in Scripture, the humble and loyal nurse of Rebekah, and the judge and prophetess who urged Barak to declare war against the Canaanites. Of the latter it is said that "she dwelt under the palm tree of Deborah." According to this Midrash the Deborah after whom the palm was named was not the prophetess but the nurse. "The palm of Deborah is the *allon bakhut* of Deborah the nurse of Rebekah."

Thus does the devoted nurse of Rebekah, first mentioned anonymously, and even when she is mentioned at her death the mourning is really for "another," finally receive the reward of her faithful lifelong service to her mistress.

floral names

VA-YESHEV. GENESIS 37–40.

> . . . *And her name was Tamar.*   GENESIS 38:6

In the portion of this week we come across the first example—possibly the first two examples—in the Bible of what has become, especially at the present time in Israel, one of the most common and universal sources of personal names, particularly for girls: the world of flora. It is common to both English and Hebrew. Among such names are Flora itself and Shoshanah (Rose) and Hadassah (Myrtle), and Tamar, to say nothing of family names, which are legion.

The one certain example is Tamar which, of course, means a date palm, and is the name of the daughter-in-law of Judah (38:6). It seems even to have become a common name in the tribe of Judah, since it was borne both by the daughter of King David (II Samuel 13:1) and by his granddaughter, the daughter of Absalom (II Samuel 14:27), and David belonged to the tribe of Judah.

The other is more doubtful and I put it forward as a mere conjecture. The wife of Judah mentioned in the same chapter of Genesis was called Bat Shua, and during the period of the Talmud there was a species of date called *benot shua* or *benot shuah*. It does not seem to be entirely far-fetched to suggest that the names of the father Shua and of his daughter Bat Shua are, like that of Tamar, connected with the date palm.

But whether the names of both Judah's wife and his daughter-in-law, or only that of his daughter-in-law, are connected with palm, the fact remains that they were the names not of Jewesses but of Canaanite women, who married into the family of Jacob. This raises the interesting question whether this custom, which has become so typically Jewish today (in Brazil there is a tradition that all girls bearing floral names are descended from Marranos!) does not have its origin in some primitive nature worship which existed among the early Canaanites.

If that should be so, it is the opposite of what appears to be the case of the only other clear example in the Bible of a girl having a floral name. For there is no doubt that, of the two names given for the heroine of the story of Purim, Esther and Hadassah (which means a myrtle), the former was her Persian name and the latter her Hebrew. And to make the contrast even more striking, there seems little doubt that the name Esther has pagan associations and is derived from the name of the goddess Ishtar, as Mordecai is from Marduk.

This is a convenient opportunity to mention one of the most interesting aspects of modern Israel and the Ingathering of the Exiles—the tendency toward the discarding of foreign names and the adoption of Hebrew ones. The movement is actively encouraged by the government, and it represents, of course, a significant and natural reversal of the well-established fact, already attested to by the Talmud, that throughout the ages Jews tended to adopt the gentile names of the environment in which they lived.

The process goes on apace in Israel, and the government publishes regularly a *Yalkut ha-Pirsumim* in which all these changes are recorded. I had occasion recently to browse through some of these lists, and the tendency to adopt names from the world of flora—flowers, plants and trees—is most pronounced.

A prime minister changed his name from Shkolnik to Eshkol, a cluster of grapes; the present deputy prime minister, born Paicovitch, is now Allon, an oak.

The new names adopted are sometimes translations, sometimes based on assonance, and sometimes have no conceivable con-nection with the previous names. Nor is the stimulus behind the change always the desire to have a Hebrew patronymic. Raḥamim, for instance, adopts the name Rimmon (pomegranate), Caleb, Carmi (my vineyard), and Yatom, Rotem (broom). And I would like to know what induced Mr. Tamar (date palm) to change his name to Brosh (cypress), while Mr. Rimoni is henceforth Mr. Allon! By adopting this name Mr. Brosh adopts a name-relationship with those who were formerly Badnarsh and Broshkowski, both of whom have made a similar change.

In this way whole "clans" are established among individuals between whom there is no other relationship. Those who before were Frei, Pirzoni, Halpern, Pikaldie, Fruchtgarten, Fruchter, Friedman, Perlstein, Rif and Prisnownik, now go under the simple name of Peri—fruit. Allon, already mentioned, seems to exercise a positive fascination. It has been adopted among many others (and the others are indeed many)—by Badisi, Yehezkiel, Alskowski, Rosenblatt, Inblitt, Rotenberg, Kahahadi, Attias, Kahalon, Mizraḥi, Alhakri and Zeuzekenbaum. Even the gentle-man whose name before conveyed wisdom—Ḥakham David—chose to change it to this name of sturdiness.

The pining after the name Pine (Oren) is evident. Lindenfeld and Tannenbaum, Einhorn and Horenliderkressler, Olmano, Ornstein, Pur, Aggi, Orhan, Yudelovski and Gelberg are all now Oren, while Erez (cedar) has been adopted and is now proudly borne by those who were previously Joseph-Ezra, Tennenbaum, Hirschmann, Yanan, Volfinski, Azdrabal and Aharanov. Shaked (almond), Vered (rose) and Vardi, Egoz (walnut) and Gafni (vine); every single name in the encyclopedia of flora has its representatives.

One could go on ad infinitum. Suffice it to sum up and say that the difficult verse (Deuteronomy 20:19), "For man is as the tree of the field," is now susceptible of a simple explanation: man in Israel calls himself by the names of trees!

BROtheRLy plants

MI-KEZ. GENESIS 41:1–44:17.

> . . . *And they fed in the* aḥu.   GENESIS 41:2

The portion of this week opens with the well-known story of the dream of Pharaoh. He dreams, and behold seven fat kine were grazing peacefully in the *aḥu* ("never saw fatter ones in my life") and after that seven thin kine ("the most impossibly thin I ever saw").

The Authorized Version of the Bible translates *aḥu* as "meadow"; the Jewish Publication Society version is "reed grass." Rashi takes it to mean a marsh, giving the Old French form of that actual word. He supports that rendering from the occurrence of the word in Job 8:11: "Can the rush grow without mire? Can the *aḥu* grow without water?" Ibn Ezra suggests that both renderings are correct, and that it means either "a valley in which grow plants" or "a specific plant." But then he goes off at a slight tangent and lays it down almost dogmatically: "But whichever of these two meanings is the correct one, the word *aḥim* in Hosea 13:15—'And he shall be fruitful among the *aḥim*'—has no possible connection with the word here, since there it means 'brethren.'" The Authorized Version agrees with Ibn Ezra and translates, "Though he be fruitful among the brethren," but while the Jewish Publication Society does not disagree with Ibn Ezra, it is Ibn Ezra who disagrees with himself! For despite his categorical statement in Genesis, in his commentary on Hosea he comments, "the word is of the same root as *aḥu* in Genesis 41:2!"

This possibility of words in Hebrew having a number of quite distinct and unrelated meanings lends a peculiar fascination to the study of the Bible. When the combination of the two Hebrew letters *alef* and *ḥet* can mean both brother and reed grass (or meadow); when in Jeremiah 36:22 it means a brazier and it occurs in Isaiah 44:16 as an onomatopoeic word, the equivalent

21

of the sighing "Ah," the homiletical and exegetical possibilities are infinite.

Nahmanides actually attempts to find a connection between the first two meanings. He takes the word in our verse to be "a generic term for all the grasses and reeds which grow by the banks of rivers and lakes" and adds, "perhaps the word is connected with *ahvah*, meaning brotherhood, because all these different species grow harmoniously side by side."

The Midrash also homiletically takes the word to be connected with brotherhood. It is only the seven fat kine who are mentioned as browsing in the *ahu*, not the thin, and it makes the sapient comment: "During years of plenty men behave as brothers to one another. That is why it states 'and they were grazing in *ahu*.' It is then that there is love and brotherhood in the world" (*Genesis Rabbah* 89:5). When all are "haves" and there are no "have-nots," strife disappears.

The suggestion, alas, can hardly be maintained. Jerome is probably right in his suggestion that in fact it is an Egyptian word, and in Akkadian *ahu* means "a river bank." How attractive it would be, however, to render the words "And they pastured in brotherhood." It suggests the peaceful browsing of these fat kine together before they were swallowed up by their lean and hungry sisters.

improving with age

VA-YIGGASH. GENESIS 44:18–47:27.

*And to his father he sent in like manner ten asses laden
with the good things of Egypt, and ten she-asses laden
with corn and bread and victuals for his father by
the way.*   GENESIS 45:23

When at last Joseph revealed himself to his brethren and sent
them back to their aged father Jacob in the Land of Israel, he
gave them all gifts, and in addition he sent his father those things
mentioned in the verse we are discussing. Asks the Talmud
(*Megillah* 16b), "What is meant by 'the good things of Egypt?'"
and answers, "Old wine, in which the mind of old men finds
comfort."

On the face of it, it sounds like a recommendation, if not
even a positive advertisement, for well-matured wine. And in
fact it is not the only place in the Talmud in which the beneficial
effects of such wine are extolled. It has even entered into the
Halakhah. In the Mishnah (*Nedarim* 9:8) it is stated that if a man
takes a vow to abstain from wine, but qualifies it by giving the
reason that "it is harmful to the bowels," he is completely
absolved from his vow, even as regards ordinary wine. This
unusual decision tends to discount the theory of the possible
harmful physical effects of wine, and it is in fact confirmed by a
fascinating story told of Rabbi Bana'ah who saw an inscription
over the gate of a city, where he was sitting as judge, which
read, "At the head of all death am I, blood; at the head of all
life am I, wine." He pointed out its inaccuracy, and the inscription
was amended to read: "At the head of all sickness am I, blood;
at the head of all medical remedies am I, wine. Only when no
wine is available have recourse to drugs" (*Bava Batra* 58b).

There seems, therefore, to be no reason to question the aptness
of the quality of old wine that "the mind of old men finds comfort
in it"—except for one point. The phrase translated "finds comfort

in it" is *noḥaḥ heimenu*. It is a standard, almost idiomatic phrase which occurs frequently in the Mishnah and other rabbinical literature but always, without exception, it applies not to physical, but to spiritual, satisfaction. (The most easily accessible passage is in the *Ethics of the Fathers* 3:13: "In whomsoever the spirit of his fellow men finds comfort [*noḥeh heimenu*] in him the spirit of the All-Present finds comfort and he in whom the spirit of his fellow men does not find comfort, the spirit of the All-Present does not find comfort." (See also *Bava Batra* 8:5, etc.)

I heard the lovely explanation that it is in fact spiritual and not physical satisfaction that is referred to here. And why? Because as the old man contemplates it he realizes that there is at least one thing which improves with age! Does not the Talmud state that "the older a scholar grows the more his mind becomes settled," and that "mind," contemplating the similar improvement in the matured wine, finds comfort in the thought.

fruitful or
fruitless

VA-YEHI. GENESIS 47:28–50 END.

. . . And his ass's colt unto the serekah *. . .*

GENESIS 49:11

The portion of this week, the last of the Book of Genesis, is dominated by the deathbed blessings of Jacob to his sons before being
gathered unto his fathers. The aged patriarch casts his gaze into the
future and tells them what will befall them and their descendants "at the end of days," in the golden Messianic Age. He speaks
to Judah, the progenitor of the Royal House of Israel: "The
scepter shall not depart from Judah, nor the ruler's staff from
between his feet" and dominion shall continue "until Shiloh
come . . ." According to the interpretation which views that
phrase as referring to the Messianic Age, the verse which follows
proclaims the blessing of that Age. It begins, "Binding his foal
to the vine, and his ass's colt unto the *serekah* . . ." And the *sorek*
vine is extolled both by Isaiah and Jeremiah.

In the Talmud (*Ketubbot* 111b), there is an ecstatic description
of the agricultural abundance of the Land of Israel, and especially
of the cornucopia of plenty which will be poured out on its
inhabitants in that blessed age. Rabbi Dimi interprets that verse
to mean: "There is not even a non-fruitbearing tree in Israel
which is not destined to produce a load of fruit which it will
take two she-asses to carry." How does the choice *sorek* become
a non-fruitbearing tree? Rabbi Samuel Edels (known as the
Maharsha, the brilliant expositor of the *Aggadot* of the Talmud)
points out that in biblical Hebrew the similar sounding letters
sin and *samekh* are completely interchangeable and virtually
identical. The three letters *samekh*, *resh*, and *kof* form the word
"*serak*," meaning empty, which is used in the Talmud particularly
for an "empty," i.e., a non-fruitbearing tree. It is upon this that
the interpretation of Rabbi Dimi is based. The *serak* will become

a *sorek*—the non-fruitbearing tree becoming one laden with fruit.

Thus does the wheel of Torah and Flora come full circle in the Book of Genesis. In his commentary to Genesis 1:11 Naḥmanides points out that according to this verse, the trees created by the act of creation were all fruitbearing trees. "And God said, Let the earth bring forth . . . the fruit tree yielding fruit, whose seed was in itself after its kind"; and in fact "the earth brought forth. . . the tree yielding fruit whose seed was itself after its kind." There was thus no provision for *illanei serak* in the place of creation and its implementation, and Naḥmanides explains that the emergence of these non-fruitbearing trees was the result of the curse on the soil after the sin of Adam and his expulsion from the Garden of Eden (3:17). That curse, however, which transformed the choice fruitbearing *sorek* into the barren *serak* would be removed in the Golden Age of the Messiah, and in that blessed age the reverse process will take place.

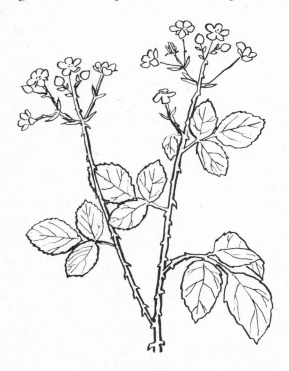

the BURNING BUSH

SHEMOT. EXODUS 1:1–6:1.

> *And the angel of the Lord appeared unto him in a flame of fire out of the midst of a bush; and he looked and, behold, the bush was burned with fire, and the bush was not consumed.*
>
> EXODUS 3:2

I very often envy the supreme self-confidence with which some biblical botanists identify some of the flora of the Bible. A tree or plant may be mentioned once and once only in the Bible, with absolutely no indication from the context as to its characteristics, yet they confidently establish its identity and proffer its learned Latin name.

In like manner, the rabbis of the Talmud were absolutely certain of the identity of some of the flora of the Bible and their identification was usually accepted beyond doubt. An example is the *s'neh*, the "Burning Bush" from which God first revealed himself to Moses, of which we read in the portion of this Sabbath.

Although the bush is mentioned on one other occasion in the Bible, and that in a most unusual context, the description of God as being "He that dwelleth in the *s'neh*" (Deuteronomy 33:16), there is absolutely no indication which would help us to identify it, apart from the miracle that "it burnt with fire but was not consumed." Yet the rabbis were certain of its identification, and the manifold details which they give of it make its modern identification almost certain. It was used in their times as a garden hedge and grows under all conditions (*Exodus Rabbah* 3:2).

It is a thorny bush whose thorns are curved inwards in such a way that "when a person inserts his hand into it he is unscathed, but when he withdraws it, it lacerates him," and the same even applies to birds which pick at its fruits. It produces a rose-like

27

flower, because of which it was sometimes called *vardina* (*Shabbat* 67a) in talmudic times. It produces a berry which is at first red but gradually turns black (Jerusalem Talmud, *Ma'aserot* 48d). It was even used as an insecticide (*Tosefta, Bava Kamma* 18:17). All these and other indications point to the correctness of the identification of the *s'neh* by the monks of St. Catherine in Sinai with the plant called, because of the incident of the Burning Bush, *Rubus sanctus*.

One detail, however, does not appear to coincide with this identification. The above-mentioned passage in *Exodus Rabbah* specifically says that it has "five petals," while the *Rubus sanctus* only has three. Professor J. Feliks, however, discovered a species of the *Rubus* in the Galilee which often has five petals, and even the formation of the *Rubus sanctus* sometimes gives the impression that it has five.

That is insofar as the botanical identification of the Burning Bush is concerned. Apart from the need to identify the flora used in religious ceremonies (e.g., the Four Species or the hyssop), however, the rabbis were more concerned with the ethical and moral lessons to be derived from the phenomena of nature than with their exact identification. In the case of the *s'neh*, one of the relevant passages is so beautiful that I allow the Midrash (*Exodus Rabbah* 2:9) to speak for itself:

"And the Lord appeared unto Moses in a bush"—A heathen inquired of Rabbi Joshua ben Korḥa, "Why did the Lord appear unto Moses in a lowly bush?" And he answered him, "And if it had been in a carob tree or a sycamore, would you not have asked the same question? But I cannot leave your question unanswered. Why in a bush? In order to teach that there is no place where the Divine Presence is not to be found, even in a lowly bush."

Rabbi Eliezer said: "As the *s'neh* is the lowliest of all the trees in the world, so Israel was reduced to the very depth of degradation before the Holy One, blessed be He, appeared to them and redeemed them."

Rabbi Jose said: "As the wood of the *s'neh* is the toughest of woods, and no bird which enters it emerges unscathed, so the bondage of Egypt was the most grievous of bondages in history."

Rabbi Johanan said: "Just as the *s'neh* is put to use as a garden hedge, so Israel acts as a protective hedge for the whole of mankind."

Another interpretation is that just as the *s'neh* can grow in any kind of water, yet water it must have, so Israel can develop only by the help of Torah which is compared to water.

Yet another interpretation: "Just as the *s'neh* grows in the garden and by the water's edge so Israel will be vouchsafed life both in this world and in the world to come."

Still another interpretation: "As the *s'neh* produces both thorns and flowers, so among Israel there flourish both the righteous and the wicked. Rabbi Phinehas ben Ḥama ha-Kohen said: Just as in the case of the *s'neh* one can insert one's hand into it with impunity, and it is only when he withdraws it that the thorns scratch him, so the Children of Israel entered Egypt in peace, and only when they had to emerge did they have to have recourse to signs, wonders and battles.

"Rabbi Judah ben Shalom said: Also, a bird can enter the *s'neh* with impunity and gets scratched only when it emerges, so the Children of Israel entered Egypt with impunity but emerged only through plagues brought upon Pharaoh."

Who shall deny the close observation of the phenomena of Nature on the part of the rabbis, and the remarkable homiletical use to which they put it?

an agricultural calendar

> . . . *And the flax and the barley were smitten, for the barley was in the ear, and the flax was in bloom. But the wheat and the spelt were not smitten, for they ripen late.* EXODUS 9:31–32

The description is given in the portion for this Sabbath of the effect of the plague of hail, the seventh of the Ten Plagues. It must have taken place about the beginning of Nisan, and from it we learn, purely incidentally, that in Egypt at that season of the year the barley was in the ear and the flax almost ripe, while the wheat and the rye had not yet formed their ears.

Forty years later, almost to the day, Joshua sent two spies to Jericho, and when their presence was reported to the king of Jericho they were hidden by Rahab in "the stalks of flax which were laid out on the flat roof of the house" for drying (Joshua 2:6). For three days the spies hid in the mountains, and three days after that Joshua crossed the Jordan, on the tenth of Nisan (4:19), at which time "the Jordan overflowed its banks all the time of the harvest," the harvest referred to there being the barley harvest.

One has only to realize that in the sunken valley of the Jordan, the Ghor, in which Jericho is situated, below sea level, crops would naturally ripen a little earlier than they do in Egypt, and one sees a striking coincidence which has been pointed out by Bishop Blunt in his *Undesigned Coincidences of the Bible*. When in Egypt the barley was in the ear and the flax bolled, i.e. the time of harvest was approaching but not yet at hand, in Jericho and its vicinity the flax had already been gathered, and the stalks were laid out to dry, and the time of the barley harvest had already arrived. Wheat, which is usually harvested about Shavuot, was

30

not yet fully grown in Egypt, and when Joshua celebrated his historic Passover, the first in the Land of Israel, "they did eat of the old corn of the land on the morrow after the Passover" (5:11) since the new harvest was not yet available.

In 1908, a limestone plaque, dating from the time of Solomon, was discovered in the ruins of Gezer. It is known as the Gezer Calendar, and it is presumed that it was used by a schoolboy for his exercises. It is a rhythmic enumeration of the agricultural seasons, not unlike the rhyming "Thirty days hath September etc." except that that jingle has nothing to do with agriculture. It enumerates the occupation of the farmer during the twelve months of the year, beginning with the olive harvest in Tishri and Ḥeshvan. These two months of the olive harvest, and the subsequent two months of planting and two months of late planting, bring us to Nisan, of which, and of the subsequent months—Iyyar and Sivan—it reads:

The month of hoeing up the flax
The month is harvest of barley
The month is harvest and festivity.

The harvests take place just a little later in the coastal plain than in the Ghor of the Jordan.

milk and honey

BO. EXODUS 10:1–13:16.

> *And it shall be when the Lord shall bring thee into the land of the Canaanite . . . which He swore unto thy fathers to give thee, a land flowing with milk and honey . . .*　　　EXODUS 13:5

No less than 19 times in the Bible is the Land of Israel referred to as "a land flowing with milk and honey." The first two references are in Exodus 3:8 and 3:17 and in this week's portion we find the third. This phrase is therefore rightly regarded as the description *par excellence* of the beautiful nature of the Land of Israel.

Most of the commentators take the description literally as referring to the bounty of the Land of Israel, both agricultural and pastoral—in the Bible honey is primarily the juice of the date, but also of other fruits; and milk, of course, belongs to the world of fauna and not of flora. The following passage from the Talmud (*Ketubbot* 112a) is a good example of that literal interpretation: Rami ben Ezekiel once paid a visit to Bene Berak when he saw goats grazing under fig trees. Honey was dropping from the figs and milk from the goats, and they mingled with one another. "This was indeed a land flowing with milk and honey," he commented.

In addition to this literal meaning, however, there is no doubt that the phrase also has a figurative meaning. The passionate lover in the Song of Songs (4:11) extols his beloved that "honey and milk are under thy tongue" and the reference is surely to the sweetness of her kisses.

Another figurative interpretation appears in the Mishnah (*Ma'aser Sheni* 5:13) to the phrase in Deuteronomy 26:15. It is to be noted that it already occurs six verses earlier where it is no doubt regarded as having its literal meaning, but here, probably in accordance with the rabbinic principle that there is no unnecessary

32

repetition in the Bible, it is interpreted as meaning "that thou mayest impart a choice flavor to the fruits."

That, however, by no means exhausts the interest of this phrase in the Bible. The first two occurrences of the phrase are to contrast the Land of Israel with the land of Egypt. In Exodus 3:8 we read, "I am come to deliver them out of the land of the Egyptians and to bring them . . . unto a land flowing with milk and honey." Nine verses later we read, "I will bring you up out of the affliction of Egypt . . . unto a land flowing with milk and honey." Egypt spelt suffering and affliction and bondage; journey's end was to be, on the contrary, a land flowing with milk and honey with its promise of joy and happiness and all things good.

It is against this background that the use of the phrase by the arch-rebel Korah and his followers and the seriousness of his revolt against Moses and his authority—the most formidable of his 40 years of leadership—are to be viewed. The rebels turn the tables. For the one and only time in the whole Bible, it is not Israel which is called "a land flowing with milk and honey," but Egypt: "Thou hast brought us up out of a land flowing with milk and honey to kill us in the wilderness" (Numbers 15:13) is the accusation they hurl at Moses. The implication is obvious. "You promised to bring us from suffering to well-being. It is just the other way around. Egypt was not a land of affliction; it was a land flowing with milk and honey, and instead of bringing us to such a land, you have brought us to a wilderness, to die miserably there."

Lastly, in one passage of the Bible the eating of milk and honey is regarded not as a blessing but as a dire calamity. In the Book of Isaiah it is foretold that the time will come when the people will eat milk and honey as part of a dire and gloomy foreboding of utter calamity. In the seventh chapter the prophet paints a gloomy picture of the utter devastation which will overtake the country as a result of the simultaneous invasion by Egypt in in the South and Assyria in the North. "The Lord shall bring upon thee, and upon thy people, and upon thy father's house, days that have not come, from the day that Ephraim departed from Judah [i.e., since the division of the kingdom], even the king of

Assyria. And it shall come to pass in that day that the Lord shall hiss for the fly that is in the uttermost part of the rivers of Egypt . . . in that day the Lord shall shave with a razor . . . the head and the hair of the feet, and it shall sweep away the beard" and so on.

The land will be laid utterly wasted; where before one thousand fruitful vines grew there will come up only briars and thorns and, incongruous though it may sound, as part of that gloomy account there comes the sentence, "And it shall come to pass, for the abundance of milk that they shall give he shall eat butter, for butter and honey shall everyone eat that is left in the midst of the land" (Isaiah 7:22).

The context makes the meaning clear. Normal agricultural activity will entirely cease; the land will revert to its primitive condition. There will be neither corn nor oil nor wine. The only things that will remain will be a few cattle ("a man shall rear a young cow and two sheep") and these animals will roam free and undisturbed, grazing on the plentiful grass and weeds which will cover the erstwhile fertile land. All that the people will have to subsist on will be the milk provided by those cattle and honey (probably bee and insect honey, gathered in the fields) and thus "milk and honey," the proverbial elements of plenty and luxury, will become the symbols of poverty, want, and hunger.

It reminds one of the possibly apocryphal story that when the people came to Marie Antoinette and complained they had no bread, she answered, "Let them eat cake."

the Desalinating tree

BE-SHALLAH. EXODUS 13:7–17 END.

> ... And the Lord showed him a tree, and he cast it
> into the waters, and the waters were made sweet.
>
> EXODUS 15:25

It is not only our present generation which is faced with the problem of water desalination. The problem is almost as old as the Jewish people. In this week's portion we read that no sooner had they crossed the Red Sea and entered the Wilderness of Shur than the problem presented itself in its most acute form. For three days they journeyed without finding water, and when at last they did come to a well "they could not drink the water of Marah for it was bitter."

But journeying as they did under Divine Providence, there was no need for Israel-American agreements on desalination plants, or for lengthy discussions as to whether atomic energy or more conventional power should be employed for rendering the water sweet. "And the Lord showed him a tree which, when he had cast it into the waters, the waters were made sweet." Tantalizingly, however, the Torah does not reveal to us the nature of this "desalination plant." What millions of pounds might not be saved were we but informed of it!

As always, the silence of the Bible on salient points constitutes a veritable challenge to the rabbis to break it. Although it is not explicitly stated, or even hinted at, the rabbis unanimously assume that it was a tree of bitter taste which was used as an antidote to the bitterness of the water. No less an authority than the Patriarch, Rabban Simeon ben Gamaliel, derives from that undisputed assumption a profound moral lesson: "Come and consider how different are the ways of the Omnipresent from the ways of mortal man. Man employs a sweet substance as an antidote

35

to a bitter one. Not so the Holy One, blessed be He; with the bitter he cures bitterness" (*Yalkut, Exodus*, 256).

Once that assumption is accepted as a fact, various rabbis put forward different suggestions in an attempt to identify the tree. These suggestions include the willow, the fig, the pomegranate root, and even trees which are not mentioned in the Bible.

If, however, the clue to the identification of the tree is to be found in its bitterness, it is obvious that a strong claim can be made out for the olive. The bitterness of the olive has become proverbial in rabbinic lore. For instance, as stated above (see *The Lesson of the Olive Leaf*), the rabbis interpret the leaf which the dove, hitherto confined to Noah's ark and deprived of its freedom, brought back to the Ark as a symbol conveying the great lesson that freedom, even if it entails privation, is preferable to its deprivation, even if it is surrounded by every material comfort.

One must therefore lend a ready and sympathetic ear to the claim of Rabbi Eleazar of Modi'in who identifies the desalinating plant with the olive, "since there is no tree more bitter than the olive."

In his recently published volume on the late Rabbi A.I. Kook of blessed memory, *The Man against the Current*, Samuel Avidor tells a delightful and moving story about the excruciating bitterness of the olive. Shortly after his arrival in Jerusalem to assume his post as Chief Rabbi, Rabbi Kook invited the *shoḥetim* (ritual slaughterers) of the capital to his house. A dish of fruit was placed before the rabbi, and to the surprise of his guests he ritually washed his hands before reciting the appropriate blessing and partaking of the fruit. In answer to the questioning look on the faces of his guests he explained, "On account of the sanctity of the Land of Israel and its produce, I have accustomed myself not to eat of its fruit without first ritually washing my hands." Whereupon one of those present, one of the oldest *shoḥetim*, by name Menaḥem Mendel, related the following story in support of the sanctity of the fruits of Israel. "When my grandfather, Rabbi Solomon Zalman of Shklov [one of the disciples of the Gaon of Vilna] came to the Land of Israel, he hired some donkeys from an Arab and proceeded to Jerusalem together with his wife and children and an old aunt who had accompanied him from Shklov. After a long and exhausting journey they at last reached the foothills of the mountains of Judea in the neighborhood of Latrun. Espying a field with shady trees they dismounted, inspected the trees and he realized that he had never seen their like before in Russia. Inquiring what they were, he was told that they were olive trees. His eyes lighted up at the realization that he had been vouchsafed to see with his own eyes one of the seven fruits which are the glory of Israel [Deuteronomy 8:8]. After being assured that they were ownerless, he gathered a handful, made the appropriate blessings, and gave some to his children. When the children bit into them their eyes filled with tears and, crying out at their agonizing bitterness, they spat them out. Sternly their father reproved them. 'Silence!' he rebuked them. 'These are the fruits of the Land of Israel. God forbid that we should be guilty of slander and say that they are bitter.'"

This lovely story adds point to the interpretation of Rabbi Simeon bar Yoḥai who denies that the desalinating plant was a tree at all! Pointing out that the word rendered "And he showed them" is from the same root as the word "Torah," he maintains that what in fact rendered the bitter waters sweet was a "word of Torah" which is "a tree of life to those who grasp hold of it." For both love of the Torah and love of the land render that which is bitter sweet.

It is nevertheless an interesting fact that there exists, and actually in the wilderness of Sinai, a desalinating plant! After the magnificent road was opened from Eilat to Sharm el-Sheikh, we toured Sinai and saw that remarkable tree. It is the mangrove. On the coast, at an oasis called Nabek, we saw an extensive grove of these mangroves growing at the water's edge. It actually draws its sustenance from the sea water but separates out the salt in the course of its growth, and the encrusted salt can be scraped off the leaves with the finger. I am even informed that in some tropical countries that deposit is actually used as a source of salt. Another of its peculiarities is that in order to inhale air its roots grow upwards, surrounding the trunk like candles on a birthday cake.

There are mangroves further south, at Ras Muhammad, on the southern tip of the Sinai peninsula, and the statement is continually made that they are the most northerly in the world. But it is not so; not only is Nabek considerably north of Ras Muhammad, but the grove there is much more extensive than that further south. In other words, they are found in the middle of the Sinai peninsula, though considerably east of Marah where the Children of Israel found the water bitter, and the desalinating tree which sweetened it.

This, of course, is a mere *jeu d'esprit*. The mangrove "desalinates" in that it absorbs and then deposits the salt. But alas, it does not "sweeten the water" and we are back where we were.

out of the ashes

YITRO. EXODUS 18–20.

ISAIAH 6:1–13 (Haftarah)

And if there be yet a tenth in it, it shall again be eaten up; like the elah *and the* allon asher be-shallekhet . . .*
ISAIAH 6:13

On the road between Ein Karem and Zova, the magnificent natural scenery has been badly disfigured: on the left one sees the glorious vista of the Hadassah Hospital topped by the two settlements Orah and Aminadav, the Kennedy Forest, and the Kennedy Monument. On the adjacent plateau one sees Even Sapir with the Monastery of John the Baptist on its lower slopes. In front is the ruined Arab village of Sattaf, and further on the right the old Arab Zuba and the Palmaḥ kibbutz Zova. But immediately on the right is the municipal garbage dump of Jerusalem!

An evil stench goes up from it during the summer months, it burns for a long period and the smell of the burning refuse adds to that of the decomposing matter. There is, however, one consoling thought. With the passage of time the vast and growing accumulation of decomposed organic matter will surely produce a rich humus which will transform the bare crags into fertile soil.

In the last verse of the *Haftarah* of this Sabbath we read of Isaiah's famous doctrine of the *She'erit ha-Peletah*, the "remnant which remains" after the holocaust. A tenth of the people shall return and they shall be "like the *elah* and the *allon asher be-shallekhet.*" These last two words are usually translated "which cast their leaves." The leaves will wither and fall but the trunk will remain and from it will emerge a new life, and in accordance with this interpretation the word *shallekhet* is employed in modern Hebrew to signify deciduous trees.

There is, however, a difficulty. Of the three species of oak

39

(*allon*) in Israel, only two are deciduous. The one which is evergreen, the *Quercus calliprinosis*, is the most common and it is strange that the prophet should take the oak as the characteristic of the deciduous tree. That difficulty disappears according to an alternative interpretation given by Rashi to this verse. After giving this "standard" interpretation he gives another in the name of the "*Poterim*," those French Jewish biblical scholars who preceded Rashi and to some extent laid the foundations of the literal exposition of the Bible. They agree that *shallekhet* means "casting" but it is not the casting of leaves of deciduous trees but the throwing out of refuse!

In the Book of Nehemiah (2:13; 3:14; 12:31) there is repeated mention of the Sha'ar ha-Ashpot, the Dung Gate of Jerusalem, as it is called to this day. It was obviously so called because through it the townspeople brought their refuse to deposit it in the valley below, probably where the Tyropean Valley meets the Valley of Hinnom (it was probably the stench and the continuous burning of the refuse which suggested that Gehinnom, the Valley of Hinnom, was the gate to Hell!). In I Chronicles 26:16, however, mention is made of the Shallekhet Gate. Since, as stated, *shallekhet* means "casting out" it is obviously identical with the Sha'ar ha-Ashpot of Nehemiah.

Rashi accordingly puts forward the attractive alternative meaning to the verse of Isaiah: "Like the *elah* and the *allon* which are in the Dung Gate." There must have stood these noble trees, flourishing all the more luxuriantly as a result of the refuse dumped there. As out of the decomposed refuse there grew these magnificent trees, so out of the destruction of the people the seed of their renewal would sprout forth again, ensuring the continuous survival of the Jewish people.

My handy biblical Concordance, published by S. Goldblum in Vilna in 1895, actually gives this translation. It is certainly a powerful metaphor and one which the emergence of the State of Israel from the destruction of European Jewry would confirm.

thorns and thistles

MISHPATIM. EXODUS 21–24.

If a man deliver unto his neighbor an ass, or an ox . . .
EXODUS 22:9

We walked through the Moshav of Aminadav on our way to Khirbet es-Said with its ruins of a Byzantine church. On one side was a garden completely overgrown with weeds, in which thistles predominated; on the other side was a neat cultivated garden in which healthy artichokes were growing.

The portion of this week deals primarily with what is called in legal terminology the laws of torts—damages for injury. On them the Midrash makes the following general comment: "With regard to every law mentioned in this chapter, whether homicide or arson or damage caused by an animal, the penalty for the transgressions is laid down, as well as the reward for their avoidance. It is like the parable of a king who made two roads. One of them was full of *kozim* and *dardarim* and brambles; the other was full of fragrant spices. Those who were unseeing walked on the bad road and the *kozim* and *dardarim* caused scratches upon scratches; those who were open-eyed, however, took the pleasant path and as they walked their garments became inpregnated with the perfumes."

The word *koz* occurs in the portion of this week without the accompanying *dardar*. "If a fire break out and catch in *kozim*." Despairingly my Encyclopaedia of the Bible declares, "There appear to be eighteen or twenty Hebrew words which point to different kinds of prickly or thorny shrubs, but the context of the passages where the several terms occur affords for the most part scarcely a single clue whereby it is possible to come to anything like a satisfactory conclusion with regard to their respective identification . . . it were a hopeless task to enter into a discussion

41

of these numerous Hebrew terms, and therefore we shall not attempt it."

That "*non possumus*" is in fact reflected in the Midrash itself which, on the words "*koz ve-dardar*" in Genesis 3:8 says: "*Koz* is the *kunras* and *dardar* the *akkavit*, though some are of the opinion that *koz* is the *akkavit* and *dardar* the *kunras*." On the other hand, the Targum, the Aramaic translation of the Bible, renders *koz* as *kubin*, prickly plants, while the *dardar* is translated as *atad*, the bramble. The only possible clue is that the whole sentence "*Koz* and *dardar* shall it [the land] bring forth and thou shalt eat the herb of the field" is taken by the Talmud (*Bezah* 34a) to mean that they are edible thorns, albeit only after a great amount of preparation. Despite this uncertainty, modern Hebrew uses the word *kunras* both for the common garden thistle and for the artichoke. They both belong to the same species, the artichoke being a cultivated variety of the thistle. As for the thistle itself, the comment of the Talmud is justified in the fact that the pith of the stalk of the thistle is definitely edible and has quite a pleasant taste. Often on our walks we pick them, peel the prickly stem and munch the pith.

And that sight on the road in the Moshav of Aminadav suggested to me a variation of the parable given by the Midrash, which would have the same moral lesson: "It is like two men who had two gardens. One left his entirely neglected; the other carefully cultivated his. In both of them *kunras* grew. But in the case of the neglected garden the *kunras* were thistles; in the other there grew delicious artichokes."

the speech of the trees

TERUMAH. EXODUS 25:1–27:19.
I KINGS 5:26–6:13 (Haftarah)

And he spake of the trees, from the cedar that is in Lebanon even unto the hyssop that springeth out of the wall.　　　I KINGS 5:13

The *Haftarah* for this Sabbath opens with the verse "And the Lord gave wisdom to Solomon as he had spoken to him" (I Kings 5:26), but the description of that wisdom precedes, instead of follows, this verse. It begins at verse 9 and includes the well-known verse which is the subject of this chapter.

The word "*al*," the preposition preceding the word "trees," literally means "upon" and whereas it is universally, in and because of its present context, translated "of," it might very well be rendered, as it is so often, "unto." Those who are by now aware of the rich and fertile poetic imagination of the rabbis, especially in their interpretation of the phenomena of nature, will be surprised, if not indeed astonished, to hear that no such interpretation is anywhere to be found in the Midrash.

But more than that. With what looks like deliberate purpose, the rabbis go out of their way to deny the possibility of speech between man and trees, or between the trees themselves. Every single verse of the Bible which might convey the impression of the possibility of such speech is carefully explained in another sense, and the rabbis flatly and categorically deny the possibility. Numerous examples could be cited, but one will suffice for the present purpose. In the famous parable of Jotham to Abimelech, which occurs in the ninth chapter of Judges, the trees are made to assemble in order to choose for themselves a king, and the discussions between the electorate and the potential candidates are given. The rabbis soberly and rationally lay it down: "It is only a parable."

It is in line with this peculiar refusal to admit of such speech that, conceding the theoretical possibility that this verse of our text might mean, "And he spake unto the trees," the rabbis nevertheless summarily dismiss it with the rhetorical question, "Is it then possible for humans to speak unto trees?" and carefully explain that it means "He spake concerning the trees, stating which of them was suitable for building, and which soil was suitable for particular trees."

There must be a reason for this strange prosaism which stands in such striking contrast to the poetry of the Midrash, and in fact it is not hard to find. The rabbis deny the possibility of speech between man and trees, and between trees and trees, in order to emphasize that the trees abandon their silence and become eloquent for one purpose only, in order to sing the song of praise unto their Creator—"Praise ye the Lord. . . fruitful trees and all cedars" (Psalm 148:1, 9)—and when they describe that speech the rabbis give full rein to their fancy.

There is, however, one remarkable exception. The talmudic sages were aware that the palm has both male and female trees and that the fertility of the female palm depends upon pollination from the male, and thereby hangs the lovely story of the passion of the Palm Tree of Jericho (*Genesis Rabbah* 41:1).

"It happened that there was a female palm tree in Emmaus, but it was barren. They grafted it, but it still refused to bear fruit. Said a certain tender of palm trees, 'That palm can see another palm in Jericho and nurses a passion for it in her heart.' They thereupon brought a cutting from it and grafted it, and it proceeded to bear fruit." And if the palm is possessed of human passions, it is also possessed of another human quality, that of speech, but apparently it was not until the ninth century that there was evidence of the manner in which that speech could be deciphered.

On two occasions the Talmud declares that among the accomplishments of Rabban Johanan ben Zakkai was his ability to understand "the speech of the date palms" (*Sukkah* 28b; *Bava*

Batra 132a). On the first of these passages Rashi, with his characteristic intellectual integrity, simply says, "I do not know what it means"; on the latter he suggested that it means that he knew all the lore about palm trees. Rashi was obviously unaware of the explanation given in the great work of his contemporary, the *Arukh* of Rabbi Nathan ben Jehiel of Rome. (The text given here, from the *Oẓar ha-Geonim* of the late Rabbi M. Levin, *Sukkah* 46, differs slightly.)

"On a completely windless day, so still that even when one spreads out a sheet it does not stir, he who understands the speech of the palms takes up his position between two adjacent palms and watches carefully how their branches incline towards one another. There is in that movement signs from which one can learn many things. And it is said of Rabbi Abraham Kabassi Gaon (who lived in the first half of the ninth century) that he was an adept in the speech of the palms, and because of that knowledge he was able to communicate great and wonderful things, the truth of which has been attested by many."

Let me conclude with a remarkable parallel. In his *Writer's Notebook*, Somerset Maugham has the following to say about his visit to Sarawak in Borneo: "At the back of the sandy shore grow the casuarinas and when the breeze stirs their lace-like foliage, they make a sound as people talking. The natives call them 'talking trees' and they say that if you stand under them at midnight you will hear voices of unknown people telling you the secrets of the earth."

If only we could interpret that speech!

olive oil

TEZAVVEH. EXODUS 27:20–30:10.

> *And thou shalt command the Children of Israel, that they bring unto thee pure olive oil beaten for the light, to cause a lamp to burn continually.*
>
> EXODUS 27:20

We have already had occasion to refer to the olive, whose oil is one of the staples of diet mentioned in the Bible, but only from one point of view—the extreme and even excruciating bitterness of the olive itself, which provides the beautiful homily relating to the leaf which the dove brought back to Noah in the Ark, and which to the rabbis provided a possible clue to the identity of the desalinating tree of Marah (see "The Desalinating Tree").

As will be pointed out, however, the interesting fact emerges that there is no reference in the Bible to the actual olive being eaten as food. Its supreme importance lay in its valuable oil, valuable because it not only was the main source of essential fats but had the added value that it could be preserved indefinitely without going rancid. But this does not exhaust its usefulness; it served as fuel for lighting, both as ointment in its pure state and as the basis for compound ointments for sacred and secular use, and it is in this week's portion that olive oil comes into its own.

This portion not only opens with the command to prepare pure olive oil for the Eternal Lamp, but also includes the details of the ceremony of the induction of Aaron and his sons into the priesthood which include the use of "unleavened bread smeared with [olive] oil" (29:2) for their anointing. Whereas, however, the oil for the lamp had to be the purest unadulterated oil, the oil of anointing, as we read in *Ki Tissa*, was mixed with powerful fragrant spices.

It is inevitable that the rabbis should compare Israel with this pure product of the olive tree which ensured that the Eternal Lamp should ever burn in the Temple, but in that comparison they are anticipated by Jeremiah, who says (11:6), "The Lord called thy name, a green olive tree, fair and of goodly fruit." But that very comparison gives rise to an objection. "Were the Children of Israel then compared only to an olive tree?" And there follows a comprehensive but by no means complete list of all the trees with which, according to them, Israel is compared in the Bible: the vine and the fig, the cedar and the walnut and the pomegranate. Why then does the prophet single out the olive? The answer constitutes a very riot of fancy in which every single aspect of the olive tree, its fruit, and its oil is pressed into service for the purpose of comparing it with Israel. Considerations of space alone permit that only the last be given in full, but it is as characteristic an example as any of the rabbis' wide knowledge of both agricultural processes and Jewish psychology.

"Just as the olive is allowed to shrivel before it is shaken down from the tree, and then it is beaten and pressed and crushed, and then ropes are tied around the vat and heavy stones placed on it, and only then does it produce its oil, so Israel, only after the gentiles come and beat them, and send them forth into exile from place to place, and bind them and tie them up, and surround them with armies, do they at last turn in repentance unto God."

But this is by no means all. Just as olive oil does not mingle with any other liquid, so Israel succeeds in maintaining its separate identity; as, when any other liquid is added to it, the olive oil always rises to the surface, so Israel will always eventually come out "on top." As olive oil is the source of light, so is Israel and so on, for "as the oil of the olive gives forth a steady light, so do the words of the Torah" (*Exodus Rabbah* 36:1, 2).

It was Upper Galilee, however, which was distinguished throughout the ages for its almost fantastic abundance of olive oil. It is already referred to, albeit indirectly, in the Pentateuch.

Twice in the Bible are the Twelve Tribes blessed, once in the last portion of Genesis, and once in the final portion of the Torah, *Ve-zot ha-Berakhah*. But the Twelve Tribes in both portions are not identical. In the first they are the actual sons of Jacob, the eponymous ancestors of what developed into the Tribes; the Blessing of Moses is to the Tribes themselves. The territory allocated to Asher was in Upper Galilee, and both the blessings make reference to the bountiful supply of olive oil which his portion would produce.

In the blessing of Jacob it is not as explicit as that of Moses, and the English translations tend to mask it. It reads, "Of Asher, his bread shall be fat, and he shall yield royal dainties," but the word *shamen* for "fat" is connected with *shemen*, (olive) oil, which was the main source of fats, and as Rashi rightly comments, "The food coming from the portion of Asher will be fat because of the plentitude of olives in it, causing the oil to flow as from a fountain."

Moses, on the other hand, explicitly states "and he shall dip his food in oil" (Deuteronomy 33:24).

The abundance of olive oil in Upper Galilee continued during the talmudic period, and in its comment on this verse the Talmud relates that once the people of Laodicea were in dire need of olive oil and appointed an agent to acquire "a hundred myriad [manehs] worth of oil." He proceeded to Jerusalem but it was in short supply there and the merchants of the capital directed him to Tyre. He met with the same reply there, and they in their turn directed him to Gush Ḥalav (the Giscala of the Roman War) in Upper Galilee. There he met a man removing the stones from the stony soil round his olive trees and he asked him whether he could provide the huge amount. "Certainly," answered the man.

The agent thought he was fooling him, but the man took him home, asked him to wait while he washed his hands and feet in olive oil, and had his meal and then, not only did he supply him with his full requirements but calmly asked him if he could do with more. When the agent said that he did not have sufficient money, the olive farmer said, "It doesn't matter, I will accompany you to your place and be paid there." He supplied him with an added 18 myriads and concludes the story, "It is said that he hired every horse, mule, camel, and ass that he could find" to transport the oil. Truly a land blessed with oil.

The abundant oil of Gush Ḥalav is reflected in the story of a man of that place who became an oil magnate, and subsequently one of the most outstanding of the fighters against Rome in the war which ended in the destruction of the Temple.

His name was Johanan and he came from Gush Ḥalav. According to Josephus, who was his mortal enemy, he was originally a poor man but amassed a huge fortune by making a corner in oil. "Pretending that he wished to save all the Jews of Syria from using oil from non-Jewish sources, he obtained leave to deliver it to them at the frontier. Then he cornered all the available supplies, paying Syrian currency worth two shillings for five gallons, and reselling it at eight times that price. As Galilee is renowned for its oil and the harvest had been exceptional, Johanan, by exploiting his monopoly and supplying large quantities, amassed untold wealth" (*Jewish War*, translation of G. A. Williamson (1959), 109).

This was, however, during the time of the Jewish war against the Romans which ended in the destruction of the Temple, and Johanan became the most formidable fighter against the Romans. He applied the huge wealth he had thus amassed to recruiting a rebel army and fortifying Gush Ḥalav. Alone of all the rebel leaders of Galilee, and unlike Josephus, the commander who deserted to the Romans, Johanan managed to extricate himself with 5,000 doughty warriors when Galilee fell and, making his way to Jerusalem, was one of the chief defenders of the capital. When Jerusalem fell, he went into hiding but was caught and taken to Rome to grace Titus' triumphal procession.

For Johanan is better known as John, and Gush Ḥalav as Giscala, and Johanan of Gush Ḥalav is none other than the intrepid John of Giscala, erstwhile oil magnate of Galilee!

Two changes, however, took place with regard to the olive and its oil in the talmudic period. The one was that the virtual monopoly of the olive as practically the sole source of oil was broken. It still maintained its position of eminence in the Land of Israel, but it was not so plentiful, or even available in other countries of the Middle East, a fact which is reflected in a Mishnah and the talmudic commentary on it.

In the second chapter of tractate *Shabbat*, which is included in the Friday night service, the various oils which are suitable for the Sabbath lamp are enumerated—sesame oil, nut oil, fish oil, colocynth oil, tar and naphtha, but of course, olive oil with its sacred associations and its ready availability was naturally preferred. The Mishnah ends with the opinion of Rabbi Tarfon that only olive oil should be used for this purpose. This brought forth a vigorous protest from Rabbi Johanan ben Nuri who rose to his feet and exclaimed: "What then shall the Babylonians do, who have only sesame oil? And what shall the Medes do who have only nut oil? And what shall the Alexandrians do who have only radish oil? And what shall the people of Cappadocia do, who have none of these and have to make use of naphtha?" (*Shabbat* 26a).

The other change is the use of the olive itself, as distinct from the oil, as a food. As stated, as far as I am aware, there is not a single reference in the whole Bible to olives being eaten as such; it is only in the talmudic period that this double monopoly of the olive was broken. Mention is made of the pickling of olives, and one species, the *Geloska*, is specifically mentioned as most suitable for pickling (*Avodah Zarah* 2:7), and in another passage the various uses to which the olive could then be put is made the basis of a moving homily in praise of proselytes: "Just as the olive produces olives for eating, and olives for preserving, and olives for oil, and it gives a better illumination than any other oil, and it is an evergreen, both in summer and winter, so out of the proselytes came scholars of the Bible and scholars of the Mishnah, men of commerce and men of wisdom, men of understanding and men 'who know a thing in its season' and their seed endures for ever" (*Numbers Rabbah* 8:10).

That metaphor of children compared to the olive is also found in the Bible. In the 128th Psalm we read of the well-being of that man "who feareth the Lord and walketh in his ways." He will enjoy the fruits of his labors; he will derive happiness and satisfaction from his wife and children. That domestic bliss is expressed in the beautiful verse which is translated, "Thy wife shall be as a fruitful vine in the recesses of thine house, thy children like olive plants round thy table."

The rendering of the Hebrew *shetilei zeitim* as "olive plants" is, however, inaccurate; one has only to observe the olive to understand the true inwardness of the simile. They are the shoots of the tree which sprout round the base of the trunk. It is the picture of the children sitting round the father at table. He represents the trunk, they the shoots.

But alas! When I told a friend of mine about it he said, "Oh, I know exactly what you mean. These are the shoots which the gardeners call *mamzerim* [bastards]." And when I sought confirmation from a gardener he said, "Yes, it is so, but we also call them *ḥazirim* [swine]!"

Thus do the legitimate children of the Psalmist become the illegitimate offspring of the slang of the modern gardener in Israel!

sinner's spice

KI TISSA. EXODUS 30:11–34:35.

> *Take unto thee sweet spices, stacte, and onycha and galbanum; sweet spices with frankincense; of each there shall be a like weight. And thou shalt make of it incense, a perfume after the art of the perfumer . . .*
>
> EXODUS 34–35

In the portion of this week we are given the ingredients and the quantities of the various spices which made up the incense used in the Sanctuary and Temple. The accepted translation is that given above.

Incidentally this list differs strikingly from that given in the Talmud (*Keritot* 6a). The passage is readily accessible, as it is included in all prayer books, and it specifically enumerates no less than eleven different species to which were added lye, Cyprus (or caper) wine, salt of Sodom, a pinch of *Ma'aleh Ashan* and, according to Rabbi Nathan, a minute quantity of the plant called Jordan Kippat. Nevertheless, the rabbis maintain that this mixture is identical with that given in the Bible, to the extent that the passage concludes, "If he omitted one single ingredient he incurs the death penalty." The manner in which they prove this identity is a fascinating example of talmudic exegesis.

In point of fact there are only two in the biblical list, galbanum and frankincense, which are identical in name with those given in the talmudic list, and from the former the rabbis derive a beautiful moral lesson which has influenced the liturgy of the most solemn moment of the most solemn day of the Jewish year, the *Kol Nidrei* service on the eve of the Day of Atonement. Although the combined effect of the mixture of spices was that it gave forth a "sweet savor to the Lord," the galbanum itself gives forth a most unpleasant odor when it is burnt. The rabbis apply this phenomenon which belongs to the world of flora to human beings. "A public fast," they declare, "in which transgressors do not participate is no fast. For though the odor given forth by the galbanum is unpleasant, it is nevertheless one of the essential ingredients of the fragrant spices of the incense offering." The recitation of the *Kol Nidrei* is preceded by a pronouncement, made in solemn fashion while three elders of the congregation each hold a *Sefer Torah* in their arms: "By the authority of the Academy on High, and by the authority of the Earthly Court, with the approbation of the Omnipresent and with the appro- bation of the congregation, we hereby declare it permitted to pray together with the transgressors."

The "transgressors" referred to in this formula belonged to a specific category. It comprised those who, because of their disregard and wilful flouting of communal enactments, were put under the ban, and thus excluded from participation in the life of the community, the only sanctions enforceable during the Middle Ages against refractory members of the community. They were completely excluded. "The banished person was not only excluded from synagogue services and other ministrations of religion, but suffered from a social and economic boycott which soon made life unbearable" (S.W. Baron, *The Jewish Community* (1947), II, 230). On this solemn occasion of the year, however, the ban was temporarily removed, and those under it were permitted to join the congregation in prayer.

The custom was apparently first introduced in Germany in the 13th century by the famous Rabbi Meir of Rothenburg whose authority was accepted by the whole of Ashkenazi Jewry. And he found a justification for it in the above-quoted passage.

A consideration of the implication of that passage brings out the tremendous message that the lifting of the ban was not so much a concession to the sinners as an appreciation of the fact that the sinners are to be regarded as an essential and integral part of the community. Because of that the author of the ritual code and commentary called the *Mordekhai*, who first mentions it, emphasizes that it was recited even if the transgressors proved obdurate and refused to request the lifting of the ban. In other words, the community needs its sinners more than they need the community.

It would be difficult to find a more striking contrast to that spirit of smug self-righteousness and the tendency to exclude the wayward members of the flock which is so prevalent today. Thus does it come about that although the offering of incense is one of the ceremonial observances of Judaism which are enjoined in the Bible but which have completely disappeared with the destruction of the Temple and have no place in our ritual observance, the spiritual fragrance induced by the thought underlying it is sweeter than all the incense in the Temple of old. Would that our souls were open to it!

Incidentally, the exact recipe for the manufacture of the incense during the period of the Second Temple was a secret which was known to one family only, the family of the House of Avtinas, and its details were handed down from father to son. They refused to accede to the request of the authorities to reveal the secret, and in an attempt to break the monopoly, the Temple authorities sent to Alexandria for skilled perfumers and instructed them to make it. The product, however, did not fulfill the requirements and not only was the monopoly confirmed, but the remuneration of the Avtinas family was doubled (*Yoma* 38a).

The early authorities strongly censured the House of Avtinas for their adamant refusal to reveal the details of the formula, but after the destruction of the Temple it was justified. The theory was advanced that the family had a tradition that the Temple would eventually be destroyed, and the reason for their refusal was that they wished to be sure that the incense would not be used for idolatrous worship. Moreover, it is stated that the womenfolk of the House of Avtinas rigidly refrained from using cosmetics of any kind lest they be accused of using the sacred incense for secular and personal purposes!

the shittah

VA-YAKHEL. EXODUS 35:1–38:20.

> . . . *And every man, with whom was found acacia-wood, brought it.* EXODUS 35:24

Because of one verse in the portion of this week I have selected it to deal with the *shittah*, the acacia, which was the only wood used in the erection of the Sanctuary, both for its furnishings and its outer walls, and I have selected the *shittah* for a more extended essay than usual, in order to illustrate in greater detail the fertile and poetic imagination of the rabbis in deriving homiletical and moral lessons from the flora of the Bible, their ability to weave fascinating legends out of the most unpromising material, and their sound botanical insight.

The legend depends upon one single word, occurring only once in the numerous references to the *shittah* in the details of the erection of the Sanctuary. Thus in the portion *Terumah* alone, the phrase *azei shittim* occurs no less than ten times; in Exodus 26:12 alone the word *omdim*, literally "standing up," is added.

This addition is made with regard to the planks which formed the outer walls of the Sanctuary and, from the literal point of view, there can be, to my mind, no shadow of doubt that the meaning is plain, namely that the planks should be made to stand upright, in a vertical position and not lengthwise, and in point of fact, this is one of the interpretations given by the Talmud: "In the manner in which the trees grow."

The rabbis were therefore by no means unaware of this plain literal meaning, and it is just this very fact which emphasizes and underlines their intention in preferring another and more imaginative and poetical interpretation. *Omdim* has another possible meaning: "ready prepared," and it is on this meaning that the rabbis develop the following lovely story.

Our ancestor Abraham was essentially a nomad and the Bible

records a considerable number of places where he took up temporary residence. Hebron and Beersheba, however, can be regarded as more or less his permanent homes and according to the Midrash he spent 25 years in the former and 26 years in the latter. That permanence with regard to Beersheba is indicated by the grove of trees which he planted there (Genesis 21:33).

But whereas Abraham was the voluntary nomad, his grandson Jacob was forced by circumstances to become the unwilling exile and it is but natural that, having finally returned to his native country, he took up permanent residence in one place, Hebron. It was from there that he sent his son Joseph on that fateful journey to seek his brethren, which was to result in his being sold as a slave to Egypt, and it was thence that 22 years later Jacob set forth with his family to take up residence in Egypt.

As we are now fully aware, after the liberation of the West Bank and the opening of the main routes hitherto closed to us, the road from Hebron to Egypt goes via Beersheba, and in Genesis 46 are informed, "And Israel journeyed with all that he had and came to Beersheba and offered sacrifices unto the God of his father Isaac." During that stopover the fateful message was given to him, "Fear not to go down to Egypt, for I will make thee a great nation there"—a gentle and euphemistic reminder of the prophecy given to his grandfather that their sojourn in Egypt would be an extended one, and that his descendants would not depart from there until 400 years from that date, and that only after great suffering.

According to the Midrash, Jacob made certain preparations for that long distant future. In Beersheba was that grove which Abraham had planted nearly two centuries before, and the trees were now, of course, fully grown. Among them were the *shittim* trees which flourish in the semi-arid climate. And in the vision of the night, according to the rabbis, Jacob was also told that when his descendants would finally emerge from Egypt and be in the wilderness they would be commanded to build a portable Sanctuary, and the timber needed for that sanctuary would be exclusively of that *shittim* wood. Since these trees were not indigenous to Egypt, Jacob made provision for that future eventuality. From the grove planted by his grandfather he took some acacia saplings and on his arrival in Egypt he transplanted them.

When, some 200 years later, the emancipated slaves who were his descendants left Egypt they took with them planks sawn from the trunks of those trees. That is the meaning of the verse, "And thou shalt make boards for the tabernacle of *shittim* wood *omdim*," "already available," as a result of the prophetic foresight of Jacob.

Of course it is only a legend, though a beautiful one; it appears to have no possible basis in the scriptural narrative and to be entirely the fruit of the rabbis' imagination. A close study of the biblical text, however, often reveals such a basis, and it is in this week's portion that such a possible basis can be found though, as far as I am aware, no one has ever drawn attention to it. In Exodus 35:24, in the account of the assembling of the materials as a preliminary to the implementation of the project, the curious verse occurs "And every man *with whom was found acacia wood* for any work of the service brought it." Thus the acacia wood was presumably not of local growth (in the wilderness!) but from stores which each one had with him. That clear suggestion that the *shittim* tree was not indigenous to the wilderness of Sinai is supported by the often repeated assertion of the rabbis, which is in fact the starting-off point of the above-mentioned legend, that in fact it was not available.

Such a fact, however, appears to be in contrast to the evidence of one's eyes. Whoever has had the opportunity to traverse the Desert of Sinai, as so many have since the Six-Day War, will surely have noticed that practically the only trees which grow in that inhospitable region, apart from the oases in the neighborhood of wells, are the stunted and gnarled acacia trees. These, together with a few *rotem* (broom or juniper), alone relieve the harsh landscape. It would therefore appear to be perfectly natural that when the Children of Israel were commanded, as we read in the portion of this Sabbath, to erect a Sanctuary in the wilderness, the sole timber which is mentioned in that connection is the *shittim* wood, acacia.

The apparent contradiction is easily resolved. It lies in the words "gnarled and stunted" which I have used in describing the acacias in Sinai. I examined tree after tree; I could not see even one which could provide even the standard-sized planks which were "twenty cubits long and one and a half wide," not to mention the "middle bar in the midst of the boards which reached from end to end" (26:28) which, as the author of the Midrash to be quoted points out, must have been 32 cubits long. Rabbi Levi, entirely eschewing the legend of Jacob's prescient planting, states prosaically: "They cut them down from Migdal Zevaya, and brought them to Egypt. And they had neither knot nor flaw in them." To that statement a fascinating historical note is added. "There still existed [in the fourth century] *shittim* trees in Migdal Zevaya, and they were regarded as forbidden for profane use because of the sanctity of the Ark [which was made from them]. The local inhabitants enquired of Rabbi Ḥanina as to the authenticity of this tradition, and he replied 'Respect the tradition of your forefathers'" (*Genesis Rabbah* 94:4). Migdal Zevaya is in the Jordan Valley near the mouth of the Yarmuk, and to this very day a small grove of the *Acacia albida*, a tall tree with thick trunk, which could have provided planks of the requisite size, grows there. Moreover, its timber is very hard, and light, and since it does not absorb moisture its volume remains constant and is suitable for construction. But it does not grow in the Desert of Sinai.

But the word *shittim* occurs also in the Bible not as the name of a tree but as that of a place, and one with ominous memories for the Children of Israel. It was in Shittim that their moral standards collapsed and they gave themselves over to revolting sexual excesses *coram publico* (Numbers 25). A 13th-century North French commentator actually maintains that, in fact, it was so called because it was from there that the Children of Israel obtained the timber for the Sanctuary. "In the wilderness," he comments, "there existed forests where grew the trees called *shittim*, and it is in fact written 'and Israel dwelt in Shittim.' It is a light, smooth and beautiful wood. It is obvious that it is a light wood since the 48 planks [made of it for the Sanctuary] together with their sockets, and bars, as well as the pillars of the courtyard and their sockets and the nine pillars of the Sanctuary with their sockets and foundations, were all carried on the eight wagons which were given to the sons of Merari for that purpose [Numbers 4:29–37], although the planks were large ones, 10 cubits long, one and a half broad and half a cubit thick. It is therefore certain that it was a precious but very light wood" (*Hizzekuni, in loc.*).

What *Hizzekuni* overlooked, however, is that the Shittim where the licentious orgy took place was not in the wilderness! The Children of Israel had already emerged from the wilderness and by their defeat of Sihon, the king of the Emorites, and Og, king of Bashan, were in possession of the fertile cultivated land of Transjordan. The existence of *shittim* trees there cannot be adduced as evidence of their existence in the desert.

The rabbis of the Midrash, however, obviously do not overlook the coincidence of the name of the place with that of the tree, but they expound it homiletically. The *Midrash Tanḥuma* to the portion *Terumah* gives a wealth of such homiletical exegesis and the rabbis proceed to expatiate in great detail on one of their favorite themes, the doctrine of compensation. The choice of *shittim* wood for the Sanctuary was to make atonement for the profanity of the Shittim place.

It is only one of the numerous interpretations to be found in that passage, and from one of them there emerges a rubric which, as far as I am aware, has never been applied in practice. "And say not that the use of *shittim* wood is confined only to the Sanctuary in the Wilderness which Moses made. Nay, in every Ark which the people of Israel make it is necessary to include a plank of *shittim* wood." It is a pity that this suggestion has not been adopted and made part of the *Halakhah* which derives from the *Aggadah*.

All that wealth of material, which is by no means exhausted by what has been written here, is in essence derived from two words, the word *omdim*, once applied to the planks of the Sanctuary, and the mention of a place called Shittim.

the pomegranate

PEKUDEI. EXODUS 38:21–40 END.

And they made upon the skirts of the robe pome-
granates of blue, and purple, and scarlet, and twined
linen.   EXODUS 39:24

Of the seven agricultural products which are enumerated as characteristic of the Land of Israel in Deuteronomy 8:8, the pomegranate is the most neglected in the Bible. In the whole of the Pentateuch it is mentioned, apart from this enumeration, only once as an actual existing fruit, and that in an almost casual and offhand manner. We are told that in addition to the near legendary cluster of grapes which the twelve spies brought back with them from their tour of the country they also brought "from the figs and the pomegranate" (Numbers 13:23). In Numbers 20:5 it is mentioned as one of the fruits which did not grow in the wilderness of Sinai. It is only in the Song of Songs, as will be seen, that the fruit and juice of the pomegranate come into their own. In the portion of this week the pomegranate is mentioned not as a fruit but as an ornamentation. The main garment of the High Priest had, attached to the hem, in alternation "a bell and a pomegranate, a bell and a pomegranate." The pomegranate referred to is, of course, not the actual fruit, but an ornament shaped like a pomegranate, made, as the Bible says, of "blue and purple and scarlet and twined linen." Nor does the pomegranate figure nearly as prominently in the homilies of the rabbis as do the other agricultural products which are enumerated with it in Deuteronomy 8:8, but there are two which are worthy of mention.

The first is one which finds virtue even in the most worthless and sinful of Jews. It says of them that "they are as full of good deeds as the pomegranate is of seed." The traditional number of commandments in the Bible is, according to the rabbis, 613 and in an idle moment I decided to put the possible truth of this homily to the test.

I had an acquaintance in South Africa who was a lecturer in mathematics at the University of the Witwatersrand. He had been taken prisoner by the Germans during the Second World War and he spent the long and weary years behind barbed wire engaged in a simple scientific experiment. It consisted of tossing up a coin over a million times and carefully recording whether it fell "heads" or "tails" in order to put to a practical test the soundness of the Law of Averages. He published his findings in a learned work, was subsequently appointed head of the Department of Statistics at that university.

I undertook a similar experiment, though a much simpler one, not in the interests of science or to prove a scientific law, but in that of Torah and Flora to gauge the accuracy of that rabbinical simile! I solemnly counted the number of pips in a number of pomegranates. I had hoped to find that the sum total was 613 or a near approximation to that number: the pips in my "test pomegranates" varied in number from a low of 404 to a high of 550. On consideration, however, I realized that I had expected too much. The optimistic view of the transgressor may make him as full of *mitzvot* as the pomegranate is of seeds, but it was not to be expected that he would be a paragon of all the *mitzvot*! And in any case, it has been pointed out that 613 represents the totality of the commandments which can be fulfilled only by all Jews collectively. Some are confined to the king, others to priests, etc., while others can be performed only while the Temple stands. This being so, my pomegranates were fuller of seeds than the number of commandments which the most observant Jew can perform. So perhaps my experiment was not entirely in vain.

The other homily is connected with one of the most dramatic incidents in the times of the rabbis of the Talmud—the apostasy of one of its great rabbis, Elisha ben Avuyah. Elisha had been the teacher of Rabbi Meir, and to the consternation of some of his colleagues, Rabbi Meir continued to meet with him and receive instruction from him even after his apostasy. How, asked the Talmud, could he allow himself to continue to receive instruction from this arch-apostate after he had abandoned Judaism, in view of the injunction that one whould study only under a teacher who is "like unto an angel of the Lord." The Talmud answers: "Rabbi Meir was different. He was like a man who eats the inside of a pomegranate but discards the peel," i.e., he was able to differentiate between what was acceptable in his master's teaching and what had to be rejected. That reply implies that the peel of the pomegranate was quite useless, but this is not in accordance with the facts. Time and again the Talmud refers to a valuable use of the peel of the pomegranate as an ingredient in dyeing.

It is, however, in the Song of Songs that the pomegranate gains prominence. The book contains the only reference in the Bible to the juice of the pomegranate (8:2), and the lover, extolling the beauty of his beloved, compares her temple to a pomegranate (4:3). But not to a whole pomegranate. The Hebrew is "like the *pelaḥ* of a pomegranate," and this word *pelaḥ* is translated in the Authorized Version as "a piece of pomegranate." The Jewish Publication Society version is more accurate. It says "as a pomegranate split open." That this is the meaning of the word is clear from the use of its verbal form elsewhere in the Bible (e.g., II Kings 4:39; Proverbs 7:23).

Only through visual observation, however, can the exact connotation of that unusual phrase be appreciated. When the pomegranate becomes overripe it splits wide open on the tree, revealing the luscious pips which are the only edible part of the fruit. It was to those pomegranates "split open" by the process of nature that the lover compared the temple of his beloved.

lots of
wood...
and walnuts!

VA-YIKRA. LEVITICUS 1–5.

*And the sons of Aaron shall put fire upon the altar
and lay the wood in order upon the fire.*

LEVITICUS 1:7

This week we commence the reading of the Book of Leviticus,
the first half of which deals at length with the various sacrifices
offered in the Sanctuary, and later in the Temple. Among all the
multifarious details which are given there is one which is passed
over in almost complete silence, namely the provision of the
enormous amount of fuel which must have been needed for the
purpose of keeping those fires burning continually, day and night,
for the 365 days of the year. All that we are told is the information
contained in the verse under discussion in this chapter, and that
the fire, as stated, had to burn continually (6:12–13), and that
the ashes had to be continually removed.

Whence, however, were these enormous supplies obtained?
It is only in the post-Pentateuchal period, and in fact, in that of
the Second Temple, that we find the answer. In the Book of
Nehemiah we read that among the various commitments which
those assembled took upon themselves at the historic gathering
called by Ezra and Nehemiah was the solemn undertaking to
provide "the wood offering, to bring it into the house of our
God . . . at times appointed, year by year, to burn upon the
altar of the Lord" (Nehemiah 10:35), and the decision as to
who would have the privilege of providing that wood was
decided by lots.

The Book of Nehemiah, however, does not reveal what were

the "times appointed" and who were the lucky winners of the lottery, and again that silence is broken by a later document which is of considerable interest. The Mishnah (*Ta'anit* 4:5) gives full details. It gives the nine "times appointed" in the year when those offerings were brought, and those who were granted this precious privilege. And one of the many interesting aspects of that Mishnah is that of the nine families or groups no less than eight of them are mentioned in the genealogical list of the families who came up from Babylon, or Persia, after the decree of Cyrus. That passage beyond question complements the passage in Nehemiah and proves that the privilege was closely guarded and handed down through the centuries between the actual lottery and the time when this Mishnah—which must of course be an early one since it deals with Temple times—was composed.

That the privilege was highly regarded is seen from a passage in Josephus' *Wars* (G.A. Williamson's translation, chapter 9). Dealing with the events preceding the outbreak of the Roman War in 66 C.E. he says: "The next day was the Feast of Wood Carrying, on which the custom was that everyone [sic] should bring wood for the altar, so that there should never be a lack of fuel for the fire that was always kept alight." From the following passage it transpires that that incident took place on the 14th of August of that year. I am sure that a calendrical expert could inform me with which of the dates given in that Mishnah the 5th, the 10th, the 15th, or the 20th of Av, August 14th coincided that year. But whatever it was, the "lots" of wood required were provided by "lots."

That is insofar as the quantities of the wood were concerned. But what quality or species of timber were used for this fuel? To that question also the Mishnah provides the answer. The consideration shown in the Bible for the preservation of fruit trees, even the fruit trees belonging to the enemy, is amply demonstrated by the passage of the Bible which forbids the cutting down of fruit trees to build a rampart against a city under siege. "Only the trees which thou knowest that they be not trees for food, thou shalt destroy and cut down, and thou shalt build bulwarks against the city" (Deuteronomy 20:20). The same principle was applied, but in a modified form, with regard to the provision of wood for the altar. The Mishnah (*Tamid* 2:3) says, "Were all kinds of wood suitable for the fire? No. All kinds of wood were suitable for the fire, except vine and olive wood. What they mostly used, however, were boughs of fig trees, and of walnut and of oleaster."

The wood was thus divided into three categories: the vine and the olive, which were absolutely forbidden; the fig, the walnut and the fig oleaster, which were customarily used; and the wood of other trees which, though permitted, were not used in practice. The Talmud (*Tamid* 29b) explains that the prohibition of vine and olive was because of their importance in the economy of Israel. And it shows a praiseworthy appreciation of the principle underlying the prohibition that those responsible applied it also to other fruitbearing and valuable trees. Rabbi Eliezer specifically adds to the list of prohibited trees the *mayish* (probably maple), the date palm, the carob, the sycamore, and the oak—a delicate tribute to its aesthetic value.

There remains, however, the problem of the fig and the walnut, which are definitely fruit trees. The Talmud answers with regard to the former that only fig trees which produced no fruit were used, while Rashi gives the lovely homiletical explanation that fig wood was singled out for burning on the altar as an expiation—on the assumption that the Tree of Knowledge of Good and Evil was the fig—and that it thereby atones for having caused primal Adam to sin.

But what about the walnut? How was it that the timber of this fruit tree was customarily used? Did it not have an economic value? A personal observation in the course of my tramps through the hills of Judea, coupled with an unusual verse of the Bible, seemed to suggest an answer.

One of the characteristics of the Arab villages in the neighborhood of Jerusalem is the existence of a single walnut tree in what is, or was, called a *bustan*—an ornamental garden. There is one, a truly noble tree, in the open space in the village of Abu Ghosh. I saw one in an abandoned Arab homestead on the lower slopes of Eitanim, another in the abandoned village of Kolonia

near Moẓa, and in some other places. The interesting thing, however, is that they are all solitary trees, and although they produce
edible nuts they were obviously planted more for ornamental
purposes than for economic reasons.

Interestingly enough this picture of the solitary walnut tree
seems to be reflected in the sole reference to the walnut tree in
the Bible. The name *egoz*, walnut, is a *hapax legomenon*, i.e.,
it occurs only once in the whole Bible (Song of Songs 6:11):
"I went down to the *egoz* garden." But the context in which
this verse occurs surely calls for some comment.

The verse continues, "to see the fruits of the valley, to see
whether the vine had flourished, and the pomegranate had
budded." In point of fact, it has been suggested that the word
naḥal in this verse, translated "valley," actually means, both
here and in Numbers 24:6, "the date palm." If this is so, then
in what is specifically called the *egoz* garden there grew date
palms, grapes and pomegranates! If it was an *egoz* garden, where
do the dates, grapes and pomegranates come in? It surely suggests
an orchard in which these fruits were the principal flora, but
it was called "the *egoz* garden" on account of the one ornamental
walnut tree which grew there. Thus do ancient biblical sources
and modern Arab usage apparently agree.

It would appear, however, that during the talmudic period,
the walnut was cultivated for commercial purposes. The Mishnah
makes mention of the shells being used for tanning (*Shabbat* 9:5)
and of their being distributed by shopkeepers to children as an in-
centive to their parents to give them their custom (*Bava Meẓẓia*
4:12). On the other hand they were extensively imported (*Tosefta,
Demai*, 1:9).

As a matter of fact the climate of Israel is generally too warm
for walnuts. Nevertheless, Josephus, in extolling the virtues and
fertility of Gennaseret, says: "Thanks to the rich soil there is
not a plant which does not flourish there, and the inhabitants
grow everything. The air is so temperate that it suits the most
diverse species. Walnuts, the most winter-loving of trees, flourish
in abundance, as do the palms which thrive in heat, side by side
with figs and olives which need a milder climate" (*Wars*, William-

son's translation, Excursus iv, 382). That assumption, however, that the walnut is not produced on a commercial scale in Israel today was disproved by the facts, and is connected with a not unamusing incident.

In an article which quoted a Midrash which compares the Jewish people, insofar as the generosity of their hearts is concerned, to three types of nuts (the hard-shelled, the medium-shelled and the soft-shelled), I quoted a letter which appeared in the Hebrew evening paper *Ma'ariv* on May 14, 1967. The wrathful reader referred indignantly to a bottle of locally manufactured brandy which he had received. It was called "Israel's Hard Nut," and according to the writer its label bore a caricature of Ben-Gurion as a walnut being squeezed in a nutcracker and resisting the pressure. "The public," he wrote indignantly, "should refuse to patronize a product which mocks in so insulting a manner one of our great national figures." I did not trouble to verify the truth of the allegation, although I confess I was puzzled by this peculiar choice of a name for a brandy. I contented myself by gently pointing out that the phrase "he is a hard nut to crack" is not generally regarded in a pejorative sense.

Some time ago I was presented with a bottle of that maligned brandy. There was on the label no caricature of B.G. as a walnut; nor was there any hint or suggestion of a nutcracker. What there was was a delightful sketch of the famous mane surrounding the top of Ben Gurion's head. And the reason for the name given to the brandy, "Israel's Hard Nut," was simply explained. It was a nut brandy . . .

On the back of the bottle was another label bearing a legend to the effect that the manufacturers "hereby certify that this brandy has been distilled from original Israeli green walnuts and from the finest wines."

Although it was perhaps reprehensible of me to cast doubt upon the accuracy of a certificate given by a reputable wine manufacturing firm in Israel, I ventured to do so in an article. Subsequently it elicited a reply from the firm informing me that in order to produce the amount of walnuts necessary for the manufacture of that brandy, they had financed the plantation of walnut orchards in two religious kibbutzim in Galilee, and the walnut crop had provided the main source of their economy. To prove the truth of that statement they actually enclosed photographic copies of the invoices for huge quantities of walnuts from these two kibbutzim.

nothing but
the best

*And the priest shall put on his linen garment, and
his linen breeches shall he put upon his flesh.*

LEVITICUS 6:3

It sounds too good a story to be true but I can personally vouch
for its authenticity. He was a wealthy self-made clothing manufacturer in Johannesburg. His wife had some pain in her finger
and he accompanied her to the doctor. The doctor stated that
it was a whitlow and that it would have to be cut open. "But,"
he said soothingly, "don't worry. It can be done with a local
anaesthetic." Upon which her husband warmly insisted on the
best imported anaesthetic! I was reminded of that story by the
fact that we are told in this week's portion that the garments
of the priest who officiated in the Sanctuary—and later in the
Temple—had to be of *bad* linen. This linen, however, is also
called *shesh*. Though the former is usually translated "linen"
and the latter "fine linen," a comparison between Exodus 28:42
and 39:28 would indicate that the two are identical. So indeed
does Maimonides maintain in his *Hilkhot Kelei ha-Mikdash*
(8:14). Abarbanel agrees, but he makes an interesting distinction.
Bad means single, and *shesh*, six. The yarn, he contends, was
called *bad*, but the thread, consisting of sextuple strands, was
the *shesh*. There is no doubt, however, that *shesh* was the name
given to the finest quality of linen which was produced in Egypt.
The first time that the word is mentioned in the Bible is Genesis
41:42 where we are told that when Pharaoh appointed Joseph
as ruler of Egypt, second only to him, he "arrayed him in vestures
of *shesh*" in token of his high office, and this is confirmed in a
letter to me by an Egyptologist, Dr. Eva Danelius, who even
maintains that it is an Egyptian word. She writes: "*Shesh* is the

70

Egyptian word for fine linen, if accompanied by the special hieroglyph. Differently written, *shs* stands for 'cord, rope'; a third hieroglyph, similarly pronounced, means 'alabaster' (the corresponding Hebrew word is used for marmor). *Shs-nsw* is the royal linen (XVIIIth dynasty) and it is possibly this kind which was purchased for the robes of the High Priests (see Gardiner, *Egyptian Grammar*, Sign-list V6, V33)." In other words *Shs* was a foreign word, like "tweed" in our days, which has been taken over into Hebrew as a *terminus technicus* for a special fabric, from the country of origin. The Bible mentions the growing of flax in Egypt (Exodus 9:31) and also in the land of Israel, in the area of Jericho (Joshua 2:6) and various varieties of wild flax grow profusely in Israel to this day. But it has always been one of the staple products of Egypt, and Ibn Ezra, in the 12th century, also maintained that of the various names given to it, *bad*, *buz* and *shesh*, it was the last which connoted the fine linen produced only in Egypt.

He adduces as evidence the verse of Ezekiel 27, which is the fascinating description of Tyre as the international "supermarket," obtaining its wares from the whole civilized world. And there it specifically mentions "shesh . . . from Egypt" not, indeed, as one of the articles of merchandise for sale, but as the material from which the sails of the Tyrian merchant ships were manufactured. Interestingly enough, in v. 16 it gives the source of the linen displayed for sale at Aram (Syria); but here it is not *shesh* but the species called *buz*. Thus, flax grew in Syria, in Israel, and in Egypt; but the pure white linen called *shesh*, used for the Sanctuary, was genuine Egyptian. The question of the linen used for the priestly garments during the period of the Second Temple is discussed in the Mishnah (*Yoma* 3:7) which deals with the Service on the Day of Atonement. The High Priest donned his garments for the Morning Service, disrobed on its completion, and then donned others for the Afternoon Service. Whereas the anonymous sages content themselves with laying it down that the morning garments were to be, or were, more expensive than those worn in the afternoon, the former costing eighteen minas while those of the afternoon cost only twelve minas, Rabbi Meir is more specific. He maintains that the morning vestments were made of linen of Pelusium, and had a value of 12 minas, while those worn in the afternoon were of Indian linen whose value was a mere 800 *zuz*.

Pelusium is the ancient name of the Egyptian Delta upon which stands Alexandria today, and it is obvious from this passage that the most expensive linen and, therefore, that of the best quality, was imported from Egypt, and used for the High Priestly garments in the Second Temple also. But apparently local Israeli linen did not even rank second. After the choice Egyptian linen, "imported Indian" took precedence over it. In other words, the local product had no showing against the "best imported."

cypRess oR sonz

SHEMINI. LEVITICUS 9–11.
                    II SAMUEL 6:1–7:17 (Haftarah)

> *And David and all the house of Israel played before
> the Lord* be-khol aẓei beroshim, *and with harps and
> with psalteries, and with timbrels, and with sistra,
> and with cymbals.*   II SAMUEL 6:5

It was David's determination to make Jerusalem not only the
political capital and the royal residence but also the spiritual center
of the Jewish people—which it has remained ever since—that
made him decide to bring the Holy Ark there from Baale-
Judah, where a generation earlier the Philistine conquerors had
taken it.

It was a joyous procession that accompanied the Ark until
the shocking tragedy took place of the death of Uzziah. A huge
and representative section of the people accompanied it with
dance and song. And David and all the house of Israel played
before the Lord with the instruments listed in the verse we are
discussing, including "*be-khol aẓei beroshim,*" literally "with
all trees of cypress," a phrase which is by no means easy to understand. How does one play before the Lord "with all trees of
cypress"? If the text is to be maintained one has to make a number
of assumptions which do not appear in that text. In the first
place one has to understand words which do not occur there,
something like "instruments made of," and in addition one
has to translate "trees" as "wood," taking "all trees of cypress"
as meaning "cypress wood." Lastly one has to assume that
cypress wood was used to make such musical instruments as the
harp, which have a wooden frame. That cypress wood was highly
valued and was used in the construction of ships is attested in
Ezekiel 27:5, and there is no reason why it should not have been
used for the fashioning of musical instruments, but that does
not dispose of the other difficulties in this verse.

All these difficulties disappear, however, in the parallel account of the same incident found in I Chronicles 13:8. The first words of the verse are identical with those of the verse in Samuel, and the first three instruments are the same as those mentioned in Samuel. For the last two, where Samuel has *mena'anim* and *zelzalim*, Chronicles has *mezaltaim*, which is obviously identical with *zelzalim*, and *hazozerot*, trumpets, for *mena'anim*, which are instruments which are "waved." And where Samuel has *be-khol azei beroshim*, Chronicles has *be-khol oz u-ve-shirim*, "with all their might and with songs." The differences in calligraphy are as small as the difference in meaning is great. But the reading in Chronicles disposes of the difficulties inherent in the reading of Samuel. So you can take your choice, Cypress or Song.

It is not the only example in the Bible in which a slight change in the text provides an entirely different meaning, but the following example is one in which a fundamental change in meaning is effected merely by the elimination of a hyphen which, incidentally, does not occur in the Bible scroll. There is a tree mentioned in the Bible called the *te'ashur*. It is mentioned in Isaiah once, in 41:19, as one of the trees which, in the Golden Age, will flourish in the wilderness, and in 60:13 as one of the trees the timber of which will be used to beautify the Second Temple when it would be rebuilt. Apart from a reference in that latter verse that it grew in the Lebanon, there are no data whereby to identify it with certainty, although it seems obvious that it is connected with a root meaning "straight" "upright." The Authorized Version of the Bible renders it "box tree," while the Jewish Publication Society version renders it "larch." All that can be said with certainty is that it is probably an evergreen and is so called because of its "uprightness."

In the 27th chapter of Ezekiel, however (v.6), there is a vivid description of the city and people of Tyre, and of the various peoples who were pressed into service to provide the materials necessary for the construction of their sea-going vessels. The masts came from the cedars of Lebanon, oars from the oaks of Bashan, the sails from the renowned fine linen of Egypt. The sailors were recruited from Sidon and Arvad, while the caulkers came from Gebal. Only the pilots, who had to know the intricate channels into the harbor, were provided by Tyre.

In that description there is a verse which is translated in the Authorized Version as "the company of Assyrians have made thy benches." The original Hebrew for the phrase rendered in translation as "company of Assyrians" is a hyphenated word "*bat-Ashurim*" and the translation depends upon regarding the first part of the word, "*bat*," as having the unusual meaning "company," while "*Ashurim*" means, of course, Assyrians.

Rashi, however, who is followed by Kimḥi, gives an entirely different rendering. According to him the hyphen is to be disregarded, and the two halves of the word to be regarded as one, i.e. "*be-te'ashurim*," with wood of the *te'ashur* tree. And the verse should be translated, "they made thy boards, gleaming as ivory [*asu shen*] with *te'ashur* wood from the isles of the Chiti'im." As a matter of fact the Jewish Publication Society translation accepts this rendering of "*te'ashurim*" and translates the verse slightly differently: "Thy deck have they made of ivory inlaid with larch, from the isles of the Kittites." And the company of Assyrians disappears and is transformed into the planks of the merchant ships of the seafaring Tyrians; as the cypress of Samuel becomes the melodious sound of song.

Before Dacron

TAZRI'A. LEVITICUS 12–13.

And when the plague of leprosy is in a garment,
whether it be a woollen garment, or a linen garment;
or in the warp, or in the woof . . .
LEVITICUS 13:47

"When Adam digged and Eve span, who was then the gentleman?" Thus ran the old rhyme which we were taught as children in school, our first steps in the doctrine of the essential equality of man. It was the popular equivalent to the impressive teaching of the Mishnah which tells us that in the adjuration which was addressed to the witnesses for the prosecution in capital charges, the judges said to them, inter alia, "Why was Adam created alone? . . to teach that no man should say, 'My descent is more honorable than yours.'"

But whereas Scripture bears testimony to Adam digging, there is none to Eve spinning. Twice the primal couple cover their nakedness, once with material from the world of flora, fig leaves, and once from that of fauna, "And the Lord God made for them garments of leather and clothed them" (Genesis 3:21).

Nevertheless, spinning was regarded as the essential domestic occupation of women both in the biblical and the talmudic periods. The most beautiful 31st chapter of Proverbs, the alphabetical poem of praise of the *eshet ḥayil*, weakly translated "the virtuous woman," includes among her accomplishments that "she layeth her hand to the spindle, and her hands hold the distaff" (v.19). The talmudic evidence is more decisive. The Mishnah (*Ketubbot* 5:5) details the domestic duties which a wife must perform for her husband. The first half of the Mishnah is strictly legal and utilitarian, reducing these duties progressively in proportion to the number of servants she brought into the marriage, with a maximum of four "if she brought in four servants she may sit [idle all day] on an armchair [*cathedra*]." This ruling, however, is not allowed to go unchallenged. Rabbi

76

Eliezer said, "Even if she brought in a hundred maidservants her husband should compel her to occupy herself with spinning, for idleness leads to moral degeneration."

But to return to the sources of materials for garments. Again it is fauna and flora which are mentioned as these sources in this week's portion, with regard to the laws of leprosy. Instead of the fig-leaf and leather, however, we have "a garment of wool and a garment of linen." And in this case the spinning or weaving is specifically mentioned, since it continues "in the warp or the woof" or, as an alternative translation has it, "in woven or knitted stuff."

Civilization progresses, and with the passage of time and the use by man of his inventive genius more and more materials are made available. During the biblical period only the three materials mentioned above were known—leather, wool, and linen. The most expensive material, in which the wealthy clothed themselves, was "fine linen," the *shesh* of the Bible (the modern theory that it was so called because it consisted of six interwoven strands is already mentioned by Rashi), or the *buz* of Esther 1:6. Its value was enhanced by its being dyed in blue or crimson or purple.

In the talmudic period other materials, deriving both from the world of flora and of fauna, became available, and the Talmud (*Shabbat* 27a) on the verse prohibiting the wearing of "wool and linen together," is able to ask, "The Scripture informs us only of a woollen or a linen garment. But what about camel hair, rabbit wool, goat's hair, silk, 'piranda silk' or corded silk?" (cf. also *ibid.* 20b). Cotton is apparently not mentioned in the Bible. And if the rabbis who discussed this matter were alive today, they would have added, "And what about dacron and terylene and nylon?"

the Rites of humility

MEZORA. LEVITICUS 14–15.

. . . And cedar-wood, and scarlet, and hyssop.
LEVITICUS 14:4

The portion of this week opens with the rites of purification of the person cured of the dread disease of biblical leprosy, the details of which are given in the previous portion.

Among the ingredients used in these rites are "cedar wood and hyssop." These two are found in combination in more than one passage of the Bible, and therapeutic or cleansing qualities were presumably inherent in them, to judge by the fact that they were also used in the preparation of the ash of the Red Heifer as well as in the purification rites of a person who had been in contact with the dead (Numbers 19:6).

The respective status of cedar and hyssop in the estimation of men, however, finds its expression in I Kings 4:33 which, describing the wisdom of Solomon, says "And he spoke of trees, from the cedar that is in Lebanon, even unto the hyssop that springeth out of the wall." Cedar and hyssop therefore represent the two extremes in the world of flora.

In a beautiful passage of the Midrash (*Ecclesiastes Rabbah* 7) this verse is used to give a homiletical explanation of the combination of these two extremes in the purification rites of the leper. Translating the opening words, as is grammatically possible, as "and he spoke unto the trees," the Midrash asks the rhetorical question: "Is it then possible for man to hold converse with trees?" and replies, "No! But this is what Solomon said, 'Why are the most majestic and the most humble of plants, cedar wood and hyssop, combined in these rites of purification? Because man is stricken with leprosy as a punishment for being haughty and arrogant as the cedar, and when he humbles himself like the lowly hyssop he will ultimately be cured.'"

It is not the only instance in rabbinic literature in which the majestic cedar is made to symbolize haughtiness and arrogance, though in the beautiful story which I am about to relate, the other extreme of humility is not the lowly hyssop but the pliant reed or bulrush which bends to the wind.

Balaam the wicked, the prototype of arrogance (*Avot* 5:22), compared Israel to a cedar (Numbers 24:5). Ahijah the Shilonite, the Hebrew prophet, apparently cursed Israel by saying, "For the Lord will smite Israel as a reed shaken in water" (I Kings 14:5). Said Rabbi Samuel ben Naḥman in the name of Rabbi Johanan, "Better the curse with which Ahijah apparently cursed Israel, than the blessing with which Balaam apparently blessed them." For "man should ever be yielding and humble as the reed, and not unbending as the cedar." And this lesson is illustrated by an incident related about Rabbi Elazar ben Simeon: As he was returning from the House of Study, full of self-satisfaction at the progress he had made in his learning, he passed by a man of exceeding ugliness, who greeted him courteously. And the sage, instead of returning the civility, said to him, "How ugly you are! Are all the people in the town from which you come as ugly as you?" To which the victim of this unpardonable rudeness answered quietly, "I do not know, but go and tell the craftsman who made me how he has bungled his job." Rabbi Elazar instantly realized the enormity of his offense, dismounted from his ass, prostrated himself before the man, and humbly begged his pardon. The other, wounded to the quick, refused to accept the apology, repeating his retort. He made his way to the city, followed by the contrite Rabbi Elazar. When he arrived there the citizens greeted the distinguished guest with the words, "Greetings, Teacher and Master." "Whom are you thus greeting?" asked the man, and when they told him, he said: "If that is a rabbi, may there be no more like him in Israel," and he told them of the gross insult to which he had been subjected by the rabbi. They pleaded with him to forgive the rabbi, and at last he relented: "For your sakes I forgive him, but only on condition that he refrains from such conduct in future."

And when Rabbi Elazar mounted the pulpit to preach, he

took as his text, "A man should always be humble as the reed and never unyielding as the cedar," and he continued, "And it is on account of its humility that the reed has been vouchsafed that from it should be fashioned the quill with which the Torah, *tefillin*, and *mezuzot* are written" (*Ta'anit* 20 a–b).

It should be pointed out, however, that the cedar, especially the cedar of Lebanon, represents not only the vice of haughtiness and arrogance, but also the virtue of majesty and dignity, as we are reminded in the Sabbath Psalm, the 92nd, in which occurs the verse, "the righteous shall flourish like the palm tree, he shall grow like a cedar in Lebanon," and the mourning *kinah* of the of the Ten Martyrs in the *kinot* of Tishah be-Av refers to them, in the opening words, as "the cedars of Lebanon."

It is possibly this double entendre which explains a curious incident related in the Talmud (*Mo'ed Katan* 25a). Rabbi Ashi asked a professional funeral orator, Bar Kipok, in what manner he would eulogize him when the time came; he answered: "If a flame among the cedars fall, what avails the hyssop on the wall?" Rabbi Ashi was so offended by Bar Kipok's poem that he gave instructions that he was not to participate at his funeral. The usual reason given for this posthumous ban is that his displeasure was due to the ill-chosen metaphor of a flame devouring him. Is it not equally possible, however, that whereas Bar Kipok, in comparing him to a cedar, intended to convey the idea of majesty and dignity, Rabbi Ashi took it as suggesting the other metaphor of the cedar, arrogance and haughtiness?

Lily among the thorns

AHAREI MOT. LEVITICUS 16–18.

> *After the doings of the land of Egypt, wherein ye dwelt, shall ye not do; and after the doings of the land of Canaan, whither I bring you, shall ye not do . . .*
> LEVITICUS 18:3

There are astonishingly few flowers mentioned by name in the Bible. In point of fact there are only two certain ones, the *shoshanah* and the *ḥavazelet* (rose?), both occurring in one verse of the Bible (Song of Songs 2:1). That the *shoshanah* is the lily is generally accepted; the suggestion that the *shoshanat ha-amakim*, "the *shoshanah* of the valleys," is not the lily, which does not grow in valleys, but the narcissus, adds one more. In addition it has been suggested, though not generally accepted, that the word *nizanim* in Song of Songs 2:12 is not a generic name for "flowers," as it is usually translated, but refers to a specific flower, the anemone. Even if all those suggestions are accepted, it brings the total to a mere four.

It is the *shoshanah* which is the subject of this article, and its connection with the portion of the week is indirect, but a perfect example of the homiletical method of the rabbis.

It is a discourse on the verse which is the subject of this chapter, and the verse chosen to illustrate it is from the Song of Songs, "As the lily among thorns, so is my love among the daughters." A number of attractive explanations is given, of which, however, only the last, as is the rabbis' wont, leads up to and connects with the chosen verse from the Scriptural reading.

"Rabbi Azariah said in the name of Rabbi Judah ben Simon, it is the parable of a king who possessed an orchard in which were planted, in successive rows, figs and vines and pomegranates and apples. He appointed a hired man to take charge of it. After some time the king came to inspect his orchard and to see how the man had performed his work, and to his dismay he found it full of thorns and thistles.

"He brought mowers to mow down these weeds but as they were fulfilling their task he suddenly espied a *shoshanah shel vered*—a rose lily—among the weeds. He took it and smelled it and, delighted by its perfume, he said, 'for the sake of that one flower I will spare the whole orchard.' So when God saw how man had spoiled the world he determined to destroy it, but when he espied one lily among the thorns, the Jewish people, who, when they were given the Ten Commandments, accepted them without even considering their implications, he said, 'Because of Israel and because of the Torah, I will spare the world as a whole.'" The metaphor thus having been applied, the rabbis give full reign to their imagination.

Rabbi Ḥanina applied the verse to Israel among the nations. Just as when the lily grows among the thorns the north wind blows it and bends it in a southerly direction and it is pierced by the thorn, and the south wind similarly bends it northwards and again it is pierced by the thorn, nevertheless, the flower still turns its face on high, so Israel is bruised by the imposts and the taxes leveled on them by the heathens, but they still direct their hearts towards their Father in Heaven, as it is written (Psalm 25:15), "Mine eyes are ever unto the Lord for he will deliver my feet from the net."

Rabbi Avin said, "Just as the *shoshanah* shrivels in the *sharav* but when the dew falls it bursts into flower again, so, as long as Esau prevails in the world, Israel appears to shrivel and wither, but in the future the power of Esau will pass away and Israel will come into its own. Just as the value of the *shoshanah* is in its scent, so Israel is justified by its good deeds."

Just as the *shoshanah* graces royal tables at all times, so Israel will endure both in this world and the next. As the lily is immediately noticeable in the field so is Israel conspicuous among the nations, as it is said, "All who see them shall acknowledge that they are a seed blessed by God" (Isaiah 61:9).

And finally comes the direct connection with the verse. Rabbi

Berechiah said, "The Holy One, blessed be He, said to Moses, 'Declare unto the Children of Israel, When you were in Egypt you were like a lily among the thorns. Now that you are about to enter the land of Canaan, continue to be a lily among the thorns. Apply your minds that you do neither according to the actions of the Egyptians nor of the Canaanites.'"

In other words, whether in the Diaspora or in the Land of Israel the Jewish people must live according to its own spiritual ideals, and the world of flora is pressed into service to teach this lesson.

But I have left to the last one lovely and unexpected additional simile: "As the *shoshanah* graces the Sabbath and Festival table, so will Israel be given the grace of redemption in the future." It is, as far as I know, the only mention in the Midrash of flowers gracing the Sabbath table.

the sycamoRe

KEDOSHIM. LEVITICUS 19–20.

AMOS 9:7–15 (Haftarah)

> *I was no prophet, nor the son of a prophet; but I was a herdsman and a dresser of sycamore-trees and the Lord took me from following the flock, and the Lord said unto me, Go prophesy unto my people Israel.*
>
> AMOS 7:14–15

It is commonly assumed by nearly all biblical scholars that Amos, the prophet from whose book the *Haftarah* of this Sabbath is selected (according to the Ashkenazi rite), was a humble shepherd and farmer in Tekoa, on the border of the wilderness of Tekoa, when the call of God came to him. The information given in the superscription that he was "of the herdsmen of Tekoa," is supplemented by the fascinating autobiographical passage which is the subject of this chapter, which is spoken to the High Priest Amaziah in answer to the edict of expulsion issued against Amos.

The sycamore, or fig mulberry, or as a local described it to me, the "Turkish fig," is comparatively common in Israel. It is sensitive to frost, with the result that it grows only in the Shephelah, the lowland, and the coastal area. This habitat of the sycamore is testified to both in the Bible and in the Mishnah. In the Bible we are told that King Solomon "made cedars as the sycamore trees that are in the valley for abundance" (I Kings 10:27), while the Mishnah (*Shevi'it* 9:2) actually makes the "sycamore line" the legal boundary between Upper and Lower Galilee.

On descending from the hill country of Jerusalem and proceeding on the main road to Tel Aviv, one first sees them outside Ramleh. Some magnificent specimens are to be seen at Ḥolon, where they are carefully preserved. That they were characteristic of the coastal area is sufficiently proved by the ancient name for what is now Haifa, Shikmonah.

The sycamore can easily be recognized by the unusual manner in which its fruit grows. Like the fig, to which it is related, the fruit grows directly from the trunk of the tree, but in little sprigs or clusters, like grapes. The fruit, when ripe, tastes something like the fig, but with a sweeter and more aromatic flavor; however, but I do not recommend to anyone to do what I did as an experiment, and eat the ripe fruit from the tree. In order to do so one must first carefully remove the many insects which have got in before! The fact is that a few days before it ripens the fruit is invariably attacked by a species of gall insect. As it bears fruit several times a year, however, and at all seasons, it was a favorite fruit for the poor, provided they were able to beat the insects to it. This they did by picking it three or four days before it ripened and puncturing it to ensure its artificial ripening. It is this operation which is usually understood to be referred to in the unique word in Amos, *boles*, translated as "dresser," and the "piercing of unripe figs" referred to in Mishnah *Shevi'it* 2:5 no doubt refers to the sycamore.

The wood of the sycamore, though porous, is very durable and is unaffected by moisture or heat. It was used in Egypt for the coffins of mummies, and they have remained unaffected through the centuries. It is the susceptibility to frost on the part of the sycamore which no doubt lies behind the suggested translation of a word in the Bible for the meaning of which there is no indication.

The bald statement in Exodus 9:25 that the plague of hail destroyed "all the trees of the field" is expanded in the poetical account in Psalms 78:47 to the effect that "He slew their vines with hail and their sycamores with *hanamal*." This peculiar word occurs nowhere else in the Bible and the exact meaning is anyone's guess, depending on the context or one's botanical knowledge. Most commentators regard it either as a synonym for hail, or as meaning locusts. Sa'adiah Gaon, however, who incidentally was born in Egypt, is the first to render it "frost." The susceptibility of the sycamore to frost is so well attested that he attributed its destruction to its greatest enemy.

Persistent attempts have been made to find a rational basis

for the ten plagues. Curious to know whether there could possibly be sub-zero temperatures in Egypt, I referred to appropriate books on the climate of that country and was intrigued to read that such temperatures have been recorded there, though at very rare intervals.

But we must return to Amos. As stated, almost all modern biblical commentators not only maintain that the prophet was a poor and humble shepherd, but they make this fact the basis of their study of him—the contrast between the simple circumstances of his life in Judah and the prosperity, based upon the exploitation of the poor, which he saw in Israel arousing his prophetic ire. The Talmud, however, takes the opposite view. It maintains that all the prophets were wealthy men of independent means and as a proof cite Amos. They regard him as the owner of sycamore plantations and, realizing that the sycamore could not grow in Tekoa, maintain that they must have been on the lowland. On this basis Rabbi Johanan (*Nedarim* 38a), in contrast to the accepted assumption that Amos was a poor herdsman, maintains that he was in fact a wealthy landowner. A person who had both flocks in Judah and sycamore plantations in the lowland was obviously a man of means.

Thus does a knowledge of botany help toward a new understanding of the Bible.

the humble Barley

> . . . *Then ye shall bring the sheaf of the first fruits of your harvest unto the priest.*   LEVITICUS 23:10

In the portion of this week there occurs the injunction to bring the *Omer*, a sheaf of barley, the first grain to ripen in Israel, to the Temple as a thanks-offering. It is, of course, the basis of *Sefirah*, or *Sefirat ha-Omer*, the counting of the *Omer* for the 49 days from the second day of Passover until the eve of Shavuot, as is mentioned in verses 15–16, and the fact that this portion is always read during the *Omer* period renders it specially topical.

Surprisingly enough, nowhere in the whole Bible is it explicitly mentioned that the *Omer* offering consisted of barley, but there is not the slightest shadow of doubt that the Talmud is correct in identifying it so, barley being the first grain to ripen in Israel, just during Passover, as anyone who travels in the country can see (*Menaḥot* 84a).

The only other reference to barley as a component of religious worship—and there it is specifically mentioned—is with regard to the offering of the *sotah*, the woman suspected of adultery. Her husband had to bring an offering which consisted of "an *ephah* of barley meal, he shall pour no oil upon it nor put frankincense on it, since it is an offering of jealousy" (Numbers 5:15; all other meal offerings consisted of pure sifted wheat flour).

The Mishnah (*Sotah* 2:1) quotes Rabban Gamaliel as giving the reason for this discrimination: "She conducted herself as an animal; let therefore her offering be of [barley, which is] animal fodder." The Talmud elaborates this statement of Gamaliel. Rabbi Meir had explained that since she had fed her paramour with the choicest and daintiest of foods, as a punishment she has to accept an offering of the coarsest food. And it was in answer to his objection that this would apply only to a wealthy

87

woman, but not to a poor one who could not afford such dainties, that the alternative explanation quoted above is given.

The factor common to both these explanations is that during the talmudic period barley was considered essentially animal fodder even though references are by no means wanting, both in the Bible and in Talmud, to its use for human consumption. That in the Bible it is indicative of poverty, is seen from such passages as Judges 7:13 and II Kings 41:12. The fact that Boaz gave Ruth merely a handful of barley is made the subject of a homily in the Midrash in which his parsimoniousness is indirectly criticized: "The Torah teaches that when a man performs a *mitzvah* he should do so with a joyous heart. . . for had Boaz known that Scripture would immortalize the fact that he gave Ruth to eat of parched [a barley] corn, he would have fed her on fatted calf" (*Leviticus Rabbah* 34:9).

But in addition to being the poor man's food it was also widely used as provender for horses, as is seen from I Kings 5:8.

In the talmudic period it was lentils that were regarded as the plainest and poorest of cereals or grain for human consumption, and this is the basis of a lovely story told in the Talmud (*Pesaḥim* 3b) to illustrate the advice that one should employ a euphemism rather than be the bearer of direct evil tidings. A certain Johanan of Hukok, a village in the north of Israel, went out to inspect his crops. On his return he was asked by the villagers whether his wheat crop had been a good one. Unwilling to tell the bad news of its failure, he answered, "The barley crop has been successful," from which they rightly deduced that the wheat crop had failed. They were none the less incensed and retorted, "Go and tell that to the horses and donkeys, as it is written, 'Barley . . . for the horses and swift steeds'" (I Kings 5:8). What then, asks the Talmud, should he have answered? And it answers that he should either have said, "Last year's wheat crop was successful," or "the lentil crop was successful," each of which would have been a more acceptable euphemism.

Despite that lowly estimate of barley, it remains as one of the seven articles of agricultural produce which are the glory of the Land (Deuteronomy 8:8). For animals have to live as well.

In some of the larger prayer books there is included an unusual chapter called *Perek Shirah*, "the Chapter of Song." It consists of a biblical verse which is attributed to every item of creation— heaven and earth, day and night, flora and fauna—in praise of their creator. It is in effect an elaboration of Psalm 148. Naturally most of the verses have a direct connection with the element which utters the praise. Thus, for instance, the palm says "the righteous shall flourish like a palm" (Psalms 92:13) and the rivers say "the rivers shall clap their hands" (Psalms 98:7). The verse for barley, however, is a cryptic one. It is "a prayer of the afflicted when he is overwhelmed and poureth out his complaint before the Lord," the superscription to Psalm 102. It is possible that the ascription of this verse to barley is a reflection of this lowly state of the "afflicted" barley in Jewish tradition to which reference has been made. To anyone who has witnessed a field of barley swaying in the wind, another, and possibly more attractive, explanation suggests itself. The word translated "he is overwhelmed" (*ya'atof*) is from the same root as that used for wrapping oneself in the *tallit*, the prayer-shawl. That field of waving barley strikingly suggests the swaying of the pious Jew, wrapped in his *tallit*, in prayer.

aBusíng the soíl

BE-HAR. LEVITICUS 25:1–26:2.

> . . . *When ye come into the land which I give you,*
> *then shall the land keep a Sabbath unto the Lord.*
> LEVITICUS 25:2

It is with a feeling of distinct spiritual unease that I consider the various halakhic legal fictions which are employed during a *Shemittah* year to circumvent the explicit laws of the Sabbatical year. The result is that whereas the letter of the law may be adhered to, its spirit, apart from its manifestation in the kibbutzim of Po'alei Agudat Israel, and even there to a severely limited extent, is entirely missing.

That spirit is clearly expressed in the biblical verse, "The land shall observe a Sabbath to the Lord . . . the seventh year shall be a Sabbath of rest to the land, a Sabbath of the Lord. Thou shalt neither sow thy field nor prune thy vineyard." The land has to rest one year in seven, as the Jew is enjoined to rest one day in seven. But advantage has been taken of a doubtful legal fiction to permit the working of the land according to the *Halakhah*, at the same tempo and with the same intensity as in normal years. (Some of my more Orthodox acquaintances have expressed the opinion that the climatic conditions which affected the crops during the *Shemittah* year 5733 are divine punishment for ignoring of *Shemittah*!)

The justification put forward for exploiting the loophole permitting agricultural activity is that with modern scientific farming methods it is quite impossible to halt agricultural processes for a year without disastrous effects to the economy, and it is this which brings me to the point I wish to make. Gradually and inexorably, almost against our will, the problem of what is loosely called ecology is being forced upon our notice. The alarming and steadily increasing pollution of the seas, the rivers, the air and the soil, which are the direct result of modern technology in all spheres, now constitutes a real danger to health and even life. And among those spheres is included just that of "modern scientific agricultural processes." The increasing use of pesticides and fertilizers is not only upsetting the balance of nature in the soil but the chemical effluents seep through to pollute the rivers and the sea. Scientists are at last beginning to study the substitution of harmful chemicals by bacteria.

Perhaps a return to the principle, if not even to the practice, of *Shemittah* would be a salutary means of restoring the balance of nature and the purification of soil and water. Refraining from the use of these chemicals for one year in seven might well result in washing out the impurities and give nature a chance to recover from the abuses to which science has subjected it. Perhaps the Almighty is wiser than we think; and it may be worth while, in the words of the prophet, to "put Him to the test."

That problem of the abuse of nature is reflected in another rabbinic dictum. In Deuteronomy 12:2 we are told that the Children of Israel were commanded that when they ultimately came into the Promised Land they were to destroy utterly all vestiges of idolatry and idolatrous worship which they would find there. But although the Bible emphasizes the utter nature of that destruction, both by the repetition of the verse and the mention of "destroying all the places wherein the nations that you dispossess served their gods, upon the high mountains and upon the hills and under every leafy tree . . . altars . . . pillars . . . graven images" etc., the Mishnah (*Avodah Zarah* 3:5) makes an exception. "If idolators worship mountains and hills, they are permitted for use, although the idolatrous objects upon them are forbidden, since the verse says 'their gods upon the high mountains'—but not the mountains themselves, and 'their gods upon the hills'—but not the hills themselves." The idea underlying this exposition is a wholesome one: nature is not to be punished for the aberrations of man. But, if so, continues the Mishnah, why does this reservation not apply equally to another manifestation of nature, and one of its outstanding glories—the spreading leafy trees, of which it is specifically stated that they had to be destroyed (these are the *asherim*)?

Could one not make the same inference, "Under every leafy

tree"—but not the tree itself! And in reply it explains that "there was human manual labor connected with these trees," i.e., unlike the mountains and the hills, they had either been specifically planted for this idolatrous purpose, or else they had been pruned and trimmed or otherwise treated, as we know these trees were, to symbolize the obscene nature of the worship which went on under them.

And again in this exception there is a wholesome and even profound underlying moral, and one which has a special lesson for us today when we are so concerned with the pollution and contamination of nature and her beauty and utility by man. For man can torture and abuse and rape nature, and so misapply its bounty that he turns it from a blessing of God to a curse. They are no longer the glorious creation of God which sing a song of praise to Him; they become the debased work of man and for their tortured souls there is but one remedy—their destruction.

the forlorn juniper

JEREMIAH 16:19–17:14 (Haftarah)

> *For he shall be like the juniper in the desert, and shall not see when good cometh; but he shall inhabit the parched places in the wilderness, a salt land and not inhabited.* JEREMIAH 17:6
> *For he shall be as a hill planted by the waters . . . and shall not fear when heat cometh but its leaf shall be green and it shall not be concerned in a year of drought, neither shall it cease from producing fruit.*
> JEREMIAH 17:8

The *Haftarah* of this Sabbath contains the beautiful passage in which the prophet Jeremiah contrasts the man who puts his trust in God with the man who does not, and he does so with a moving floral simile. The *Ethics of the Fathers* applies these verses to another contrast, between the man who prefers knowledge to good works and vice versa. The undesirable one is 17:6 while 17:8 is the desirable one.

The word translated "juniper," *ar'ar*, is rendered "heath" by the Authorized Version of the Bible, and "tamarisk" by the Jewish Publication Society version. There is hardly any doubt, however, that the New English Bible is correct in rendering it "juniper," since the juniper is called *ar'ar* in Arabic also.

Juniper has smuggled its way, in disguise, into the English language. The alcoholic liquor known as gin is also called "geneva" (of which "gin" is a contraction). "Geneva" is not a place-name but a corruption of the French *"genièvre"* which, in turn, is derived from the Latin word *"juniperus,"* the juniper tree. The liquor was so called because the juniper berry is used in its manufacture. And so the moralist who may not be averse to a "gin and tonic" or to a "gin and it" may even soliloquize in rabbinic vein: "Thus it is that even the juniper in the desert, which is taken as the simile of all that is bad and undesirable, may be put to good use," or find here just another example of the oft-repeated comment of the rabbis that there is none so bad but has some redeeming feature in him!

The word *ar'ar*, however, occurs in another verse of the Bible: "He will regard the prayer of the *ar'ar* and not despise their prayer" (Ps 102:18). There is a beautiful and moving comment on this verse in the Midrash, "Said Rabbi Isaac, This verse applies to the generations of the future [after the destruction of the Temple], to that era when there will be neither prophet nor priest who shall serve as the Teacher of Righteousness, nor the Temple which shall atone for the sinners. All that will be at their disposal will be one solitary prayer which they will utter on Rosh Ha-Shanah and Yom Kippur. O Lord, despise us not, as it is said, 'and despise not their prayer.'"

What is the meaning of this word *ar'ar* in this verse? With a rare unanimity, all the standard versions of the Bible—the Authorized Version, the Jewish Publication Society translation and the New English Bible—render it "destitute." The word, however, belongs wholly and indubitably not to the human world but to the world of flora, as has been seen from the passage in Jeremiah.

And it is the juniper, that forlorn and unhappy lonely denizen of the parched places of the desert, which stands in contrast to the tree which symbolizes the man who puts his faith in God: "A tree planted by the water which spreadeth out its roots by the river, that shall have no fear of the burning heat, but its leaf shall ever be green and shall have no anxieties in the year of drought, neither shall it cease from bearing fruit."

It must be that selfsame metaphor which the Psalmist has in mind when he prays to God not to despise the prayer of the *ar'ar*, and it is that metaphor which is in the mind of the author of the Midrash quoted above. Man, his protective fence of smug self-satisfaction down, realizing his frailty, conscious that he has cut himself off from the life-giving waters of the Torah, sensing the aridity which has eneveloped his soul, tasting the bitter taste of the "salt land," comprehends that there is no vicarious atonement for him, neither "prophet nor priest nor Temple," but only a single prayer that breaks forth from his contrite soul. It is all that he has left, but surely it will not be despised, for "He despiseth not the prayer of the *ar'ar*."

And to that metaphor, modern Hebrew has added a new dimension. For if in the Book of Psalms the *ar'ar* is a person and in Jeremiah a tree or shrub, in modern Hebrew its root means "to lodge an appeal." And if the prayer of the forlorn and destitute is not answered on Rosh Ha-Shanah, Jewish theology maintains that there is an opportunity for *ar'ar*, for appeal, on the Day of Atonement!

nicholas dates

BA-MIDBAR. NUMBERS 1:1–4:20.

> *Bring the tribe of Levi near*, etc. (3:6). *Thus it is written: "The righteous shall flourish like the palm-tree* (Psalm 92:13) ..." NUMBERS RABBAH 3:1

Moshe Dayan is known to be an unconventional personality, and is reputed on occasion to disregard the niceties of the law. In his fascinating biography of Dayan, Shabbetai Tevet gives an example: his raiding of fowl pens and of orchards during his military service. One of these exploits happened during the heat of the Sinai Campaign in 1956. On November 3, he arrived in El-Arish which had just been captured by our forces in order to give instructions for the speedy resumption of normal life there. Tevet continues, "Despite the late hour when the conference concluded, Dayan did not forego a visit to the date plantations there. After he expressed his astonishment at the manner in which they grew in the sand dunes and expressed his amazement at their freshness—'Neither in Beth Shean nor on the banks of the Kinneret have I seen such fresh and luscious dates'—and after helping himself there on the spot, and taking some for the journey, he returned to Tel Aviv."

Had I been there on that occasion, I might have asked him, "I wonder whether these dates are as choice as the *nikalvasin* of the Talmud," for the *nikalvasin* were also a choice species of dates, and the name is also intimately connected with the political history of the Jewish people.

On the portion of this Sabbath, the Midrash compares Israel to the date palm. It gives numerous comparisons between the qualities of the tree and its fruit and the qualities of the people of Israel. I confine myself in this chapter to one such comparison only. "Just as the palm tree produces *nikalvasin* and an inferior quality of dates which drop from the tree when unripe and prick, so among Israel there are educated persons as well as ignoramuses and boors."

The *nikalvasin* which, from the context, are obviously the finest quality of dates, are referred to in the Mishnah (*Avodah Zarah* 1:5). The word means simply "Nicholas dates," and thereby hangs a fascinating story of one of the most colorful characters who lived during the period of the Second Temple.

Nicholas of Damascus was a well-known Greek philosopher and historian. He was not a Jew, nor apparently did he ever become converted to Judaism. Possessed of considerable wealth, he had no need to seek a means of livelihood, nor did he have any desire to seek honors. He became closely attached to Herod the Great, and took up his residence in the royal palace. There he remained, in Jerusalem, for 20 years faithfully and loyally serving his self-appointed royal master. He accompanied the king on all his various journeys to Rome and to Asia Minor, and on one occasion was sent by him to Rome on a successful mission of intercession on behalf of Herod to the Emperor Augustus.

Herod used to indulge in philosophical discussions with him and, realizing his talents, he encouraged him to write his monumental history, consisting of no less than 144 books. This history has a special interest for us. It was, according to the accusation of Josephus, a slanted history. In order to remove from Herod the reproach of his non-Jewish descent from the Idumeans, who were forcibly converted to Judaism by John Hyrcanus, he invented a new genealogy for him, making him a descendant of a noble Jewish family of Babylon. In fact, Josephus maintains that the whole purpose of the history was to glorify Herod, "making a pompous encomium upon what just actions he had done, but earnestly apologizing for his unjust ones."

During his visits to Rome he gained the esteem of the Roman Emperor Augustus, and it is expressly stated that, on hearing that the Emperor was especially fond of choice quality dates, he kept him supplied with a special variety which grew particularly in the Land of Israel. In appreciation of their provider, the Emperor bestowed upon them the name "Nicholas dates." These are the *nikalvasin* of Mishnah and Midrash, to which Jewish scholars are compared.

the nazirite

NASO. NUMBERS 4:21–7:89.

> *He shall separate himself from wine and strong drink
> and shall drink no vinegar of wine; neither shall he
> drink any liquor of grapes, nor eat grapes, moist or
> dried. All the days of his separation he shall eat
> nothing that is made of the vine tree, from kernels
> even to the husk.* NUMBERS 6:3–4

The portion for this week includes the law of the Nazirite (*Nazir*
in Hebrew), the person who took a voluntary vow of abstention,
including wine. A reference to the relevant passage which is
the subject of this chapter, however, reveals that this last prohibition was much more comprehensive than mere abstention
from wine.

The deprivation was therefore more than a denial of self-
indulgence. It is impossible to exaggerate the literally vital role
played by the vine and its products in the food basket of biblical
times. The following brief extract from a fascinating essay by
Dr. Menashe Harel serves to indicate that importance:

"The fruit of the vine was of great importance, thanks to its
many uses. Fresh grapes were served as food, yet their food value
was even greater when dried as raisins, which can be preserved
even in desert conditions . . . An additional use of the grape was
for making jelly preserves, a great delicacy in the East. However,
the most important use of the vine was in wine manufacture
. . . Wine was a vital necessity, being preserved in earthen-
ware jars in times of peace and times of emergency. The an-
cients also produced vinegar out of the wine. This they used
as a food seasoning, since it improved the appetite by stimulating
the gastric juices in the burning days of summer. It also served
as a vegetable preservative."

It is probably in the light of this that the remarkable comment
of Rabbi Simeon bar Yohai in the Talmud is to be viewed. Dis-

regarding the plain meaning of verse 11 which refers to the sin committed by the Nazirite who broke his vow by contact with the dead, he regards it as referring to the actual Nazirite vow, which he considered as "a sin against the soul." And he makes the interesting comment, "If this man who took a vow to abstain from wine [and its products] only is regarded as a sinner against his soul, how much more so from all the permitted pleasures of life!"

Thus in that abstention from wine he deprived himself not only of the pleasures of life but of something which was a vital necessity in those days. That this is the inner meaning of the prohibition would appear to be confirmed by one fact which is not generally appreciated. The prohibition against wine by the *Nazir* is not to be understood as teetotalism, and according to the *Halakhah* a *Nazir* could theoretically become "drunk as a lord" providing that he confined his alcoholic beverages to those from products other than grapes. If, on the one hand, the prohibition extends to the vine and all its products, even non-alcoholic ones, it does not extend to alcoholic liquors produced from other fruits, and the Nazirite could indulge in such potent liquors as vodka, kummel, arak, and saki!

This fact is reflected in the Targum, the "official" Aramaic translation of the Bible. The prohibition begins with *yayin* and *shekhar*. These two names also occur in juxtaposition in the prohibition against priests officiating in the Sanctuary (Leviticus 5:1). That prohibition, however, is obviously an injunction against the priests officiating while in a state of intoxication, irrespective of the source of that intoxication. The Targum therefore translates the two words there "wine and all intoxicating liquors," whereas, in the case of the Nazirite it translates them "[new] wine and old wine."

Despite the condemnation, or at least discouragement, of the rabbis of persons taking the Nazirite vow, cases of Nazirites were nevertheless not unknown, and in 1967 there was accidentally discovered on Mt. Scopus the most ornate funerary vault yet discovered in the Jerusalem area, outdoing that of the family of Herod. It dates from the first century C.E. and the inscription on it shows that it was the burial place of Jonathan the Nazirite, his wife (whose name is not given), his son Ḥanania and Ḥanania's wife, Salome. The last two names, however, were found only on ossuaries on the site.

Only two sarcophagi were found, a large one (200cm. × × 57 × 51) and a smaller one (188cm. × 45 × 42), and it was natural to assume that the larger was of the lord and master, while the smaller was of his anonymous spouse. That assumption is strengthened by a striking difference between the two. The larger one is plain and unornamented while the smaller is richly decorated with blossoms, leaves, and clusters of grapes.

To adorn the grave of a Nazirite with grapes would be an outstanding example of transgression against the law known as "lo'eg la-rash" (mocking at a poor man), since he voluntarily forbade himself the products of the vine. But his abstinence was obviously not shared by his wife.

It is interesting to note that the law of the Nazirite explicitly includes the possibility of a woman taking on a Nazirite vow; it is introduced by the words, "a man or a woman." There are at least two outstanding instances of women becoming Nazirites. The first is the mother of Samson, as related in the Haftarah of this Sabbath. The other is of the most distinguished of all women converts to Judaism in the time of the Second Temple, Helena Queen of Adiabene in the first century C.E. In the Mishnah (Nazir 3:6) it is related: "It once happened that the son of Queen Helena went to war, and she said, If my son returns safely I will be a Nazirite for seven years. At the end of the seven years she came to the Land of Israel and the school of Hillel told her that she must be a Nazirite for yet another seven years. At the end of that second seven years she contracted uncleanness. Thus she continued to observe her Nazirite vows for 21 years."

egyptian salad

BE-HA'ALOTKHA. NUMBERS 8–12.

We remember the fish, which one did eat in Egypt free of charge, the cucumbers and the melons and the leeks and the onion and the garlic. NUMBERS 11:5

In this week's portion we read of the hankering of the Children of Israel after what they claimed were the pleasures of the palate which had been theirs in Egypt. They had already expressed their yearnings for the transient "fleshpots of Egypt" (Exodus 16:3). But now they yearned for the more homely comestibles which made up their diet. The verse we are discussing as quoted above is the translation given in the standard versions of the Bible, and I confine myself in this article to three words: the *dagah*, translated "fish," the *ḥazir*, translated "leeks," and the *bazal*, the "onion." With the possible exception of the *dagah*, all these products belong to the world of flora and, indeed, to vegetables, and it is germane to the subject of this chapter to note that the reference is to vegetables which grew in Egypt. Of the five, *avatiaḥ* ("melons"), *bazal* ("onion"), and *shum* ("garlic") are mentioned only here in the Bible. So are *kishu'im* ("cucumbers"), except that in Isaiah 1:8 the word *mikshah*, a cucumber patch, is mentioned, while the last *ḥazir*, although it is extensively mentioned elsewhere in the Bible, has an entirely different meaning there.

Let us begin with the *ḥazir*, translated in this verse as "leeks." The word, as stated, is of frequent occurrence in the Bible, but in the other passages it bears a meaning quite different from what it does in our verse. Whereas here it is quite certainly an edible vegetable, and "leeks" is as good a translation as any, elsewhere in the Bible, however, and relating to its provenance in the Land of Israel, it refers to grasses, and even the rankest of grasses, which are suitable only as animal fodder, edible herbs usually being referred to as "*esev*." Instances could be given without number, but two will suffice. The first is the verse in I Kings 18:5 in which, during the famine which raged in the land, the king Ahab instructed Obadiah to "go into the land, unto all the sources of water and unto all brooks, perhaps we may find *hazir*, to save the horses and mules alone, that we lose not all the beasts." The clearest and most cogent evidence, however, is afforded by the beautiful Nature Psalm, the 104th. The rains run down from the hills, with the result that "He causeth *hazir* to grow for the cattle, and *esev* for the service of man, that he may bring forth food out of the earth . . . wine . . . oil . . . and bread." It is obvious that these five products are mentioned in the order of ascending importance and value, the *hazir* being the lowest of all, and it gives rise to a homely comment of the rabbis, to which I hope my many readers who belong to the gentler sex will not take too violent exception, especially in view of the grudging concession with which it ends. "There are three things which man does not desire, *hazir* in his standing corn, girls as his children and his wine turned to vinegar. But the world has need of all of them, and it is in reference to that that this Psalm opens with the words, O Lord God, thou art exceeding great" (*Tanhuma*, *Hayyei Sarah*). And so *hazir*, insofar as it refers to a humanly edible vegetable, is distinctly Egyptian.

And so is the onion! Throughout the ages Egypt has been extolled for the quality of its onions. In ancient times both Pliny and Herodotus made specific mention of the fact that in their their time the onion was a favorite and staple article of food among the Egyptians. And although since that time it has become one of the most widespread vegetables in the world, with Spanish onions being regarded as the finest variety, the preeminence of the Egyptian variety has often been attested. I came across the following passage in a traveler's diary written over a century ago: "Whoever has tasted onions in Egypt must allow that none can be better in any part of the universe. Here they are sweet; in other countries they are nauseous and strong . . . they eat them roasted . . . with some sort of roasted meat which the Turks in Egypt call kebab. With this dish they are so delighted that I have heard them wish they might enjoy it in Paradise!

Indeed, it is even possible that in ancient Egypt the onion was—deified!"

The inspired architect of the Sanctuary erected by the Children of Israel was Bezalel ben Uri. The Midrash beautifully interprets the name as meaning *"be-zel El"*—"in the shadow of God"—a lovely reference to artistic inspiration. That, however, is a purely homiletical interpretation, and when I received a letter from one of my readers as to the possibility of the name being connected with *bazal*, I was inclined to reject the suggestion out of hand as absurd. And yet, after consideration, I am not so sure. Prof. Feliks takes the name Bazluth in Ezra 2:52 as being derived from this root. If so, Bezalel could possibly be a theophoric name, like Nathanel or Elhanan, and would mean "Divine onion!" Is it indeed a fantastic suggestion? The *bazal* is Egyptian, and Bezalel was born in Egypt. And I was intrigued to read that in ancient Egypt the onion with its concentric skins was regarded as symbolizing the planetary system, and according to Pliny (*Natural History* 9:16) it was even an object of worship, some even swearing by its name.

And lastly, to the apparent non-flora item in the food basket of Egypt for which the Children of Israel hankered—the *dagah*, translated "fish." It is true that the word *dagah* is a generic name for fish, and is found in the Bible with regard to the fish in the Nile which died in the Plague of Blood, also in Egypt (Exodus 7:21). But the claim that the slaves in Egypt were provided with fish free of charge has puzzled many commentators. The *Sifre* even goes so far as to deny the truth of that plea entirely, a typical exaggeration in order to bolster up their complaint. "Is it possible," argues the *Sifre* cogently, "that when they were denied straw for making bricks, they should have been given free issues of fish?" Ibn Ezra regards the word as referring merely to the cheapness of fish.

The most interesting suggestion, however, comes from the Tosafists' commentary on the Bible, *Da'at Zekenim*. Pointing out that in Genesis 48:16 the verbal form of the word *dagah* means to increase, and giving the French equivalent of *"croissance"* for the word, they maintain that the word does not mean "fish" at all, but is a comprehensive and generic word for agricultural produce and increase of the fields, of which the individual items which follow are the particularized details.

The "fish" in the verse therefore disappear and from fauna they are turned into flora, and the verse is to be rendered, "We remember the bountiful supplies of the produce of the field which we ate in Egypt, the cucumbers and the melons and the leeks and the onions and the garlic," which certainly gives a more balanced meaning.

If that interpretation is accepted, is it necessary to adopt the ingenious etymology of the Tosafists? Cannot the word *dagah* be taken as an alternative form of *dagon* which means "corn"?

a coincidence of dates

SHELAH LEKHA. NUMBERS 13–15.

> *. . . Now the time was the time of the first-ripe grapes.*
> NUMBERS 13:20

The portion of the week opens with, and is dominated by, the story of what are loosely called "the Twelve Spies." We are told that they went "in the days of the firstfruits of the grapes," but that vague date is pinpointed by the Talmud (*Ta'anit* 29a) as being the 29th day of the month of Sivan (cf. Pseudo-Jonathan to this verse). In point of fact it is towards the end of the month of Sivan that the bountiful harvest of grapes is available in plenty in the fruit shops and on the stalls in the market, and apart from the fact that there is a gap of time between the "days of the first fruits of the grapes," and the full harvest, one might assume that this determination of the date was influenced by the fact of the grape season. But it is not so. There is another interesting possibility as to the reason for this determination, if not actually for the 29th of Sivan, then at least during the last week of that month. The portion *Ba-Midbar* is always read on the Sabbath preceding the festival of Shavuot. Shavuot falls on the 6th of Sivan, and since *Shelah*, the portion which includes the incident of the spies, is the fourth portion after *Ba-Midbar*, the 29th of Sivan must of necessity fall in that week in which the portion *Shelah* is read. Yet even that is merely a coincidence.

The real reason for positing that day as the day of the departure of the spies is based upon quite different considerations. They returned from their exploratory journey "at the end of forty days"; and on the morrow they gave their pessimistic report which was to have such dire and disastrous consequences—the postponement of the entry of the Children of Israel into the Promised Land for 40 years. According to the rabbis, that fateful day was none other than the Ninth of Av, the Day of National

Mourning, and it was that act of faithlessness on the part of both the ten spies and the people which established it as the destined day for "*bekhiyyah le-dorot*," of "weeping for future generations." On this basis the day of their return was the eighth of Av, and in point of fact the same Targum actually renders the verse "at the end of forty days" as "on the eighth day of Av, the fortieth day after they set out." A simple calendrical calculation establishes that, if so, the day that they set out was on the 29th of Sivan, and this date exactly coincides with the period of the ripening of the grapes in the area where the spies saw them. There is, however, one difficulty.

According to the scriptural narrative, the day was "the period of the first-ripe grapes," while at this period of the year we are in the midst of the full harvest. It is, of course, possible that the harvest had fully ripened during the period that they were away. But there is no need to have recourse to this explanation. When I visited Hebron on a conducted tour, our knowledgeable guide informed us that the Hebron area is particularly famous for a certain grape and it is the latest grape to ripen in the Land of Israel.

Thus do the agricultural seasons of Israel, the timetable for the reading of the weekly portions, and the homiletical teachings of the rabbis completely coincide.

The first of these considerations, however, is equally relevant to the other fruits which the spies brought back. The near-fabulous and almost legendary cluster of grapes which has become a double symbol in Israel today, both of the famous Rishon le-Zion wine cellars and of the Ministry of Tourism, looms so large that it has virtually masked the fact that these grapes were not the only agricultural products of Israel which they brought back with them.

The Bible specifically mentions that, in addition, they brought back "of the figs and of the pomegranates." But not only are these other products put in the shade, so to speak, by that huge cluster of grapes; the offhand manner in which the Bible adds them, almost as an afterthought, gives the impression that they did not rank in importance or impressiveness with the grapes.

There is a sound agricultural reason for this distinction. Of the seven agricultural products of Israel enumerated in Deuteronomy 8:8, and called in the Talmud "the glory of the Land of Israel," five are fruits. They are, in order, figs, grapes, pomegranates, olives, and dates.

At the end of Sivan, of these five fruits, only the grapes are fully ripe. Figs and pomegranates ripen later in July or August. As for olives and dates, they do not ripen until as late as October or November.

The spies obviously wished to bring samples of the agricultural wealth of Israel. Only grapes could be carried in their fully ripened state and the biblical account emphasizes this. As for figs and pomegranates, these fruits were only half grown, but sufficiently advanced to be exhibited. This is, of course, the reason for the clear distinction in the manner in which they are mentioned as compared with the grapes. Olives and dates, however, are not sufficiently developed in Sivan even for their embryonic stage to be seen, and they were therefore not included in the display of "the fruit of the land."

the ROD OF aaRON

KORAH. NUMBERS 16–18.

> *. . . And, behold, the rod of Aaron for the house of Levi was budded, and put forth buds, and bloomed blossoms, and bore ripe almonds.* NUMBERS 17:23

There is a curious passage in the Talmud (*Bekhorot* 8a) which equates the parturition of various animals with the time that it takes for certain fruits to attain ripeness after their blossoming. To give some instances: "The dog goes with young for 50 days, and corresponding to it is the fig which produces its fruit in the same 50 days; the 52 days of the cat corresponds to the 52 days of the mulberry; the 60 days of the pig to the same period for the apple tree."

The list is given according to the length of the periods, and the first is the hen, which lays its eggs after 21 days, corresponding to the 21 days from the blossoming of the almond tree to the ripening of its fruit.

This process, rapid though it is, cannot, of course, be compared to the story of Aaron's rod of which we read in this week's portion. Overnight it budded and brought forth buds and bloomed blossoms and yielded almonds. But even the 21 days call for comment. It is proverbial (cf. Jeremiah 1:11) that the almond is the first tree to blossom in Israel; and Tu bi-Shevat, the New Year for Trees, invariably sees the blossom already on the tree. In point of fact, Rashi in his commentary on the verse of our portion quotes a homiletical explanation of the miracle of Aaron's rod based on this early blossoming. Says Rashi, "Why the almond? Because it is the first tree to blossom. So does calamity come speedily upon all who rebel against the priesthood." The Midrash is much more original. The rabbis compare almost every tree and plant in the Bible to Israel; the vine and the fig and the olive and the date and the walnut, etc., etc. In this instance, however, their comment constitutes an example of what is called in Yiddish *"punkt fehrkert"*—"just the other way round." Says the Midrash, "Why was the almond chosen of all trees for the performance of this sign and miracle? Why not a rod of pomegranate or of walnut? Because a tree was chosen to which Israel is *not* compared." But the statement that 21 days later the fruit is ripe appears to be questionable. If the almond gets off to a quick start it does not maintain this pace and it is not until around Tishah be-Av, six months later, that the nuts are ripe.

The explanation is, however, simple. The reference is not to the ripening of the nuts but to the green almonds, which are eaten whole, and which are a great delicacy to Oriental Jews. They are already on sale in the market toward the end of Adar, and are a favorite delicacy on Passover. There are thus two ripenings of the almond, the first 21 days after the blossoming, and the second and full ripening of the nuts around Tishah be-Av. These two facts are combined in a Midrash which again makes the point that the almond's period of ripening is 21 days; but it compares three weeks to the Three Weeks of mourning from the 17th of Tammuz to Tishah be-Av.

But the legend of the Rod of Aaron does not end there:

The Mishnah in the *Ethics of the Fathers* (*Avot* 5:9) enumerates ten things which were "created on the eve of the Sabbath [of Creation] in the twilight." On that passage, the late Dr. J.H. Hertz quotes the lovely statement of Israel Zangwill: "The Fathers of the Mishnah in stating that . . . were not fantastic fools but subtle philosophers, discovering the reign of universal law through the exceptions, the miracles that had to be created especially, and were still part of the order of the world, much as apparently erratic comets are."

Among them is "the Rod of Moses," i.e., the rod with which he performed his miracles in Egypt. To the "unanimous" list given there, however, there are various additions, introduced by the words "some say," and among them is "the Rod of Aaron, complete with its flowers and almonds." The addition does not appear in the "supplementary list"—the printed editions of the *Ethics*; it is, however, mentioned in the oldest rabbinic commentary on the Bible, the *Mekhilta*, and it was included in the version of the *Ethics of the Fathers* referred to by the 12th-century French commentator on the Bible, Hezekiah ben Manoah. In his commentary, known as the *Hizzekuni*, he comments: "The Rod of Aaron produced flowers—the reference is to the *Pirhei Kehunnah*, the flowers of the priesthood, who were the priestly cadets in the period of the Second Temple, and it produced almonds [*shekedim*], a reference to the eagerness [*shekedim*] with which the priests were wont to carry out their duties in the Temple. That is why the *Ethics of the Fathers* includes the Rod of Aaron among the things created on the eve of the Sabbath." Truly it appertains to the near miraculous that not only should the priests always be on their toes in fulfilling their sacred functions, but that there should always be eager aspirants to succeed them.

Despite the fact that the Bible expressly states that the Rod of Aaron was "to be kept as a token against the rebels, and Moses did so" (v. 24), there is no further mention of it in the Bible. That veil of silence, however, is lifted by the rabbis.

That same passage of the *Mekhilta* includes "the Rod of Aaron, complete with its flowers and almonds" among the things which the prophet Elijah is destined to restore to the Children of Israel in the Messianic Age, "as it is said, 'Restore the Rod of Aaron'" [Numbers 17:25]. But when was it lost? According to the Talmud it was, in fact, zealously preserved in the Temple until the time of the king Josiah. Foreseeing the forthcoming Destruction of the Temple, however, he hid it away, together with "the vessel containing the manna" (Exodus 16:33) and that containing the "water of sprinkling" of Numbers 19:19 (*Yoma* 52b); "And that Rod is destined to be in the hands of the King Messiah—may he come speedily in our days!—as it is said, 'The Lord shall send the rod of thy strength out of Zion: rule thou in the midst of thine enemies'" (*Numbers Rabbah* 18 end).

ceдar, кíng or commoner

And the priest shall take the cedar-wood, and hyssop, and scarlet, and cast into the midst of the burning of the heifer.   NUMBERS 19:6

In the chapter "The Rites of Humility" on the portion *Meẓora* we dealt with the combination of the *erez*, usually translated "cedar," and hyssop in religious rites. The same combination occurs again in this week's portion in the preparation of the ashes of the Red Heifer, used for the purification of the person who had become ritually unclean through contact with a corpse. It is the basis of the rabbinic homily which, dependent on the combination of the most majestic tree in the world of flora and the humblest of plants, extols the virtue of humility.

That homily depends upon the identification of the *erez* with the famed Cedar of Lebanon, which is variously taken to symbolize either majesty or arrogance. It is, however, by no means certain that the *erez* always refers to this tree.

A study of the connotation of the word "*erez*," both in Bible and in Talmud, makes it clear beyond doubt or question that the word is employed in two distinct senses. It is applied to one specific and distinctive tree, the magnificent Cedar of Lebanon, the very King of Trees; it is equally used in a generic sense for a whole group of non-fruitbearing trees; in other words, the *erez* is both king and commoner. The evidence insofar as the Bible is concerned seems clear, though it cannot be said to be conclusive. It is to be found in Psalm 148, in which all of creation is called upon to join in a chorus of praise to its Creator, and in the world of trees the call is extended to "fruit trees and all *arazim*," a juxtaposition which surely seems to include all non-fruitbearing trees under that general name.

In the Talmud, however, the evidence is altogether decisive and conclusive. A passage in the Babylonian Talmud begins by stating that there are four trees to which the name *erez* applies, the *erez* itself, the *kedras*, the pine, and the cypress. The *erez* is the cedar, the word *kedras* is the actual word cedar, and since the pine and the cypress are conifers, on the basis of this passage one might conclude that the term refers to this species only.

The passage, however, goes on to quote another rabbi who maintains that there are no less than ten species of *erez*, which include the seven trees mentioned in Isaiah 41:19 and rendered—some inaccurately—in the Authorized Version as "acacia, myrtle, oil-tree, cypress, plane, and larch." To them the Talmud adds the oak, the bay tree, and the carob.

The most extensive enumeration is found, however, in the Midrash (*Exodus Rabbah* 33:1) and it is of interest to give it in full. "Rabbi Samuel ben Naḥman stated in the name of Rabbi Jonathan, 'There are 24 species of *erez*. Of them seven are of special importance, as it is said "I will give in the wilderness" followed by the seven trees mentioned in Isaiah 41. And why were they not hidden away [from the sight and use of man, but reserved for the delight of the righteous in the world to come]? Because the Holy One, blessed be He, foresaw that they would be needed for the erection of the Sanctuary where His divine Spirit would dwell!'"

As has been pointed out in the chapter "The *Shittah*," the only wood mentioned in the erection of the Sanctuary is the *shittah*, the acacia, which is in fact among the seven enumerated by Isaiah, yet the Midrash consistently regards it as synonymous with *erez*.

The evidence is therefore conclusive. As to what group of non-fruitbearing trees it refers there is a difference of opinion. Low in his classical *Die Flora des Juden* is of the opinion that it includes all evergreens, while Moldenke, in his *Plants of the Bible* limits it to trees which grow in rich and fertile soil. This gives point to the prophecy of Isaiah that in the Messianic Age they will grow in the desert wastes.

As stated, to the rabbis, the Cedar of Lebanon symbolizes

two possibly complementary and possibly opposing qualities, majesty and arrogance. The rabbis expatiate on the former quality in their comment on Psalm 9:12, "The righteous shall flourish like the palm tree, he shall grow like the cedar in Lebanon." They claimed it, so to speak, as their own, and made its qualities symbolical of the righteous man, of the Children of Israel as a whole, as well as of such worthies as Jacob and David: "As the cedar has many roots, so that if even all the winds of the world blow they are powerless to uproot it, so the power and actions of David are before the Holy One, blessed be He. Even though all the nations of the world combine against him they are powerless to move him from his place" (*Yalkut, Psalms* 845).

The cedar with whom the lowly thorn wished to intermarry (II Kings 14:9) was none other than Jacob (*Genesis Rabbah* 14:9) and so on. Its virtues are extolled, its beauty expatiated upon, its qualities applied to all moral virtues; in short it is the perfect tree. But, as has been seen (see "The Rites of Humility"), they are equally eloquent in their symbolization of the cedar as the representative of haughtiness and arrogance.

CEDARS OF LEBANON.

a garoen By the euphrates

BALAK. NUMBERS 22:2–25:9.

> *As the valleys they are spread forth, As gardens by the river side, As the aloes which the Lord hath planted, And as the cedar trees beside the waters.*
>
> NUMBERS 24:6

The most famous prophecy of Balaam, the heathen seer who was hired to curse the Children of Israel, but who remained to bless, is that verse which has entered so massively into our liturgy, particularly as the opening verse of the order of service on all special occasions. "How goodly are thy tents, O Jacob, thy dwelling places, O Israel." That paean of praise is followed by a less well-known verse, which is translated above.

Of the four similes cited—"valleys," "gardens," "aloes" and "cedars"—of only one, the second, is the translation unquestioned and no alternative has ever been put forward. Of all the other three, however, the accepted translation has been called into question, and it has been suggested that the *nehalim* are not "valleys," the *aholim* not "aloes," nor the *arazim* "cedars"! The correct rendering of *arazim* not as "the cedar" but as "non-fruitbearing evergreens" has already been dealt with in the previous chapter, and it, of course, disposes of the difficulty upon which the rabbis based their beautiful homily on the virtues of humility, namely that the cedar (of Lebanon) does not grow by the waters, but at high mountain altitudes.

With regard to the *nehalim* translated as "valleys"—itself a forced translation, since the word usually means "a brook,"—it has been pointed out that the word *nahal* in Arabic is used for the palm tree, and it almost certainly has this meaning in Song of Songs 6:11, which should be rendered not "I went down into the garden of nuts to see the fruits of the valley," but "to see the sprouting palm," which is followed by "and to see whether the vine has flourished and the pomegranates budded." This translation provides the attractive and beautiful rendering of our verse, "Like palms majestically rearing their heads [stretched out]." Lastly we come to the *aholim*, translated "aloes." I am convinced that the rendering is correct, but it happens that no less an authority than Immanuel Low, the brilliant and usually completely reliable father of biblical botany, does not accept this identification, on the grounds that the aloe does not grow in the Land of Israel. And for that sole reason he identifies it with another plant.

In so doing he makes an all too common mistake, namely to assume that all the plants in the Bible grew in the land of the Bible.

What, indeed, could Balaam, whose home was in "Pethor, which is by the River," and who journeyed from there to Moab, know of the flora of Israel? It is surely obvious that he was influenced in this beautiful simile by the manifestations of nature in his own country, and I have followed the example of the Jewish Publication Society translation by spelling River with a capital R (22:5), since it undoubtedly refers to *the* river *par excellence* of the East, "the great river, the Euphrates." The river to which he compares Israel is the Euphrates, and the gardens are those growing on its banks. The Targum Onkelos realizes this and actually renders the second line, "As gardens by the Euphrates." There the majestic palms raised their heads; there the aloes grew, and on its banks the various evergreens spread their leafy branches. And in his ecstatic vision he saw in all these beautiful manifestations of nature a simile of the excellence of Israel.

the Rotem

PINḤAS. NUMBERS 25:10–30:1.
                I KINGS 18:46–19:21 (Haftarah)

But he himself went a day's journey into the wilderness, and came and sat down under a rotem *tree . . .*

I KINGS 19:4

In his flight from the vengeance of Jezebel to Mt. Horeb, where he is vouchsafed the tremendous vision of the Lord not in the fire, or the tempest or the earthquake, but in the "still, small voice," Elijah the prophet, at the end of a long and weary journey of a whole day in the wilderness, rests under a *rotem* tree. There, in his utter despair at his failure after the dramatic encounter with the prophets of Baal on Mt. Carmel, he begs God to take his life, and lies down to sleep. During that slumber an angel touches him and tells him to awake and eat, "And he looked, and behold, there was a cake baked on the coals, and a cruse of water at his head."

The *rotem*, translated in the Revised Version as "juniper," is actually the broom, the *Retama roetam*, and although an angel does not necessarily have to have recourse to the normal domestic means of cooking, there is a close connection between the *rotem* and the coals upon which the cake was baked. In Psalm 120:4 the deceitful and false tongue is compared to "sharp arrows of the mighty with coals of *rotem*," and to this day the Bedouin, in the absence of all other fuel, employ the hard wood of the broom and its root for fuel and charcoal.

The point of the metaphor is explained by the Talmud and Midrash. If the "sharp arrow" refers to the immediate effect of the piercing and wounding malicious gossip, inflicted from a safe distance, the "coals of *rotem*" refer to its lingering effect. In the Talmud (*Bava Batra* 74b) Rabbi Huna ben Nathan relates that he once roasted a leg of mutton on *rotem*—charcoal in the desert, and on returning to the spot twelve months later he found the charcoal still glowing. To that the Midrash (*Genesis Rabbah* 98:23) adds that "whereas all other coals retain their fire externally while they are extinguished internally, *rotem* charcoal, though the fire may appear dead on the outside, still glows within," and it concludes with the statement that a fire of *rotem* kept burning for eighteen months, "a winter, a summer and a winter."

The other mention of the *rotem* in the Bible—Job 30:4—raises a problem, since it refers to the edibility of the root of the *rotem*. Not only is the root so bitter as to be quite inedible, but it is even poisonous. It has therefore been suggested that the phrase is to be taken to mean "the eating of food prepared by roasting on the root of the *rotem*."

There is a possible reference to the *rotem* in the Pentateuch. Among the various encampments of the Children of Israel in their forty years' wandering in the wilderness in Numbers 33, there is one called Ritmah. "And they journeyed from Hazerot, and they encamped at Ritmah. And they journeyed from Ritmah." The name Ritmah seems obviously connected with the *rotem*, the broom, which grows extensively in the wilderness, and in point of fact the Pseudo-Jonathan Targum to the verse renders it explicitly, "Ritmah, a place where the *rotem* grew in profusion." A. Berliner, in his note to his classical edition of Rashi, actually says, "The place is called today Wadi Gaian and the *rotem* grow there in profusion."

Rashi, however, goes a stage further. Probably influenced by the fact that although Ritmah is enumerated in the list of encampments, it does not appear in the actual narrative of the wanderings, he maintains that its real name was not Ritmah. It was a nickname given to it by the Children of Israel. And why Ritmah? "Because it was there that the spies gave their evil report of the Land of Israel, since slander is compared to the *rotem* tree, as it is said [Psalm 120:4], 'What shall be done to thee, thou false tongue? Sharp arrows of the mighty with coals of *rotem*.'"

What on the surface appears to be a mere *jeu d'esprit* on the part of Rashi is cogently justified on rational grounds by one of his classical supercommentaries, the *Siftei Hakhamim* of Shabbetai Kohen. He points out that in the detailed historical narrative of the journeyings of the Children of Israel, as given in Numbers 12:16, the encampment which was the stage of their journey after Hazerot is not Ritmah but the Wilderness of Paran ("And afterwards the people journeyed from Hazerot and they encamped in the Wilderness of Paran"). Thus the geographical name of the place was Paran, and Ritmah a mere nickname. It was in Hazerot that Aaron and Miriam were guilty of the slander of their brother Moses (cf. Numbers 11:35 and 12:1); it was immediately after that that the incident of the Twelve Spies took place. It was a period of moral degeneration, of slander, evil reports, lack of faith. And that moral is summed up in the suggestion that the Children of Israel came to refer to it not by its real name, but by that of Ritmah, the place of the *rotem* which symbolizes the Evil Tongue.

the Desert and the Sown

MATTOT. NUMBERS 30:2–32:42.
    JEREMIAH 1:1–2:3; 2:4–28; 3–4; 4:1–2
                                    (Haftarot)

> . . . I remember for thee the affection of my youth, the
> love of thine espousals. How thou wentest after me
> in the wilderness (ba-midbar) in a land that was
> not sown.   JEREMIAH 2:2
> . . . The Lord that brought us up out of the land of
> Egypt; that led us through the wilderness (ba-midbar)
> through a land of deserts and pits, through a land of
> drought and the shadow of death, through a land that
> no man passed through, and where no man dwelt.
>   JEREMIAH 2:6

When the two portions *Mattot* and *Masei* are read separately
the *Haftarah* of the first portion is Jeremiah 1:1–2:3; when they
are combined, the *Haftarah* is the following passage, Jeremiah
2:4–28; 3:4; 4:1–2. It is the only instance of two successive
prophetic portions being read on two successive Sabbaths. It
does not affect the choice of the verse for this discourse, since its
subject is the *midbar*, and the *midbar* occurs in both passages,
though with a different connotation. In Jeremiah 2:2 there
occurs the beautiful passage which is included in the *Musaf*
service of Rosh Ha-Shanah. Four verses later there is another
reference to the wilderness, the *midbar*. The prophet complains
of the ingratitude of the people of Israel, their forgetfulness of
the divine boon.

The first *midbar* is merely "a land which is not sown," it is
arable land which needs only water to make it fertile, and the
only reason that it was "not sown" was because of the lack of
water. It was this *midbar* which was the grazing ground for the

flocks of sheep and goats; it was this *midbar* to which Moses led the flocks of Jethro his father-in-law in Midian (Exodus 3:1); it was there that the youthful David was supposed to be tending his sheep when, to the anger of his eldest brother Eliab, he came to the battlefield (I Samuel 17:28).

Well do I remember the first time that fact was brought home to me. It was during my period of military service in North Africa during the Second World War. From the outskirts of Alexandria to the Libyan border was an almost unbroken stretch of desert. But on the army maps the area was marked "arable," and that this designation was accurate was proved by one interesting fact. A temporary camp would be established, and outside the mess tent a trestle table set up on which, among other things, vegetables were cut up. When the table was washed down after use, the seeds would fall on the ground and the water would cause them to germinate and flourish.

Thirty years later I had occasion to refer to another instance of this arable *midbar* which was "not sown" merely because of the lack of water, and the transformation when water was made available, and it included the following passage:

The surprise of the soldiers who crossed over to the west bank of the Suez Canal during the Yom Kippur War and saw the flourishing and fertile fields on that side of the Canal, in striking contrast to the bare waste on the other side, gave rise to a definite exaggeration. "A veritable Paradise," "a Garden of Eden," they reported enthusiastically. To me, whose fate it had been to have my headquarters in that area for nearly two years during the Second World War, when I was Senior Chaplain to the British Army in the Middle East, it was clear that they would soon realize the truth.

It was a noisome, pestilential area, teeming with flies and bugs and other insects, and the water was infested with bilharzia. Nevertheless, the fertility was a fact; waving palms, mangoes and limes and oranges, maize fields and gamoose. It was the the direct result of a simple fact. The Sweet Water Canal which had been dug prior to the cutting of the Suez Canal and running its length, primarily to provide water for the laborers on the

Canal, was subsequently used for irrigation for the felaheen who established farms and villages in the area.

In other words, the mere existence of water can literally turn the desert into a garden and, needless to say, the reclamation of the Negev is another example of that "arable *midbar*."

But in addition to this, and distinct from it, is the geological formation which we are accustomed to associate with the word "wilderness, desert," the harsh inhospitable conditions of most of Sinai which is so vividly described in the second passage; the "land of deserts and pits, the land of drought and the shadow of death, the land that no man passes through and where no man dwelt."

the caper

MASEI. NUMBERS 33–END.

> . . . *To give the inheritance of Zelaphhad our brother*
> *unto his daughters.* NUMBERS 36:2

The caper bush flourishes luxuriously throughout Israel. Although, as will be clear in the course of this chapter, it was cultivated in talmudic times, it only grows wild today. It figures with almost undue prominence in rabbinical literature, but in the Bible it has only two doubtful references. The one is in the beautiful last chapter of Ecclesiastes which depicts in metaphorical language the gradual waning of man's physical powers until "the pitcher be broken at the fountain and the wheel broken at the cistern" and "the dust returned to the earth as it was." It includes the verse "and the *aviyonah* shall fail." In the Authorized Version of the Bible the word is translated "desire," the reference being the decline of man's physical desires and passions which come with old age. The Jewish Publication Society translation, however, follows modern scholars who regard the word as having the same meaning as it has in the Mishnah which will be referred to later, namely, the "caperberry," and the reference is merely to the jaded appetite which is not roused by the piquant caper! Personally I prefer the other translation.

The second doubtful reference is to be found in this week's portion, where the personal name Zelaphhad appears. Among the many names for the caper found in the Talmud, the most common is *zelaf*. "Had" in Hebrew means "sharp," and as anyone who, like myself, gathers the buds and the fruit of the caper for pickling knows to his cost, one of the characteristics of the caper bush is its wicked sharp thorns. Ephraim Ha-Reuveni, the pioneer of what may be called "local" biblical botany was apparently the first to suggest that the name Zelaphhad actually means "sharp caper," and in this he has largely been followed by later Israeli botanists; he even gives an imaginative explanation of this name of the father of the five brotherless daughters. The modern name for the plant, caper, is derived from the Greek *kapparis*, which occurs in the Mishnah, and all these three names, the biblical *aviyonah*, the talmudic *zelaf* and the Greek *kapparis* are found together in one Mishnah (*Ma'aserot* 4:6) which states "Rabbi Eliezer says, from the *zelaf* tithes must be given from the *tamarot* [usually translated 'the young stalks,' but I am of the opinion that it refers to the flowers, which are edible and which, indeed, spread out like miniscule palms; thus the name *tamar*], the *aviyonah*, and the *kapparis*. Rabbi Akiva says, only the *aviyonot*, since they are its fruit." (Incidentally, it is from this passage that it is certain that in Mishnah times the caper was cultivated, since only cultivated plants are liable to tithe.)

There is a veritable *embarras de richesse* in the many references to, and stories about, the caper in the Talmud and Midrash, and it is with some regret that I must limit myself to only a few.

There is a passage in the Talmud (*Bezah* 25b) which enumerates the *azim*, the "strong ones" in the world; for instance, the lion in the animal world, and Israel among the nations. A supplementary suggestion is "the caper among shrubs." The reference is undoubtedly to the toughness and virility of this plant which produces an almost inexhaustible and recurrent supply of buds, flowers and fruit (which remarkably enough can be seen altogether on the shrub at one and the same time) despite the fact that it grows in the stoniest of soil and in the interstices of stones. It may, however, also refer to the piquant taste which has made it such a widespread and favorite condiment, a characteristic which influenced the modern translation of the word in Ecclesiastes, and according to Rashi, and to my mind he is undoubtedly right, this pungency is referred to in another passage.

There is a passage in the Talmud (*Keritot* 6a) known from its opening words as "*Pittom ha-Ketoret*," which is included in the liturgy. It gives the ingredients of the incense which was used in the Second Temple, and includes "three *se'ah* and three *kabs* of *kafrisin* wine, but if *kafrisin* wine was not available, one could substitute old white wine." It concludes with another reference to this *kafrisin* wine, to the effect that the *onycha*, another ingredient, was steeped in it that it might be *azzah* (strong, pungent).

All the modern authorities translate "*kafrisin* wine" as "wine from Cyprus," despite the fact that it is at least passing strange that when wine was abundant in, and one of the main agricultural products of Israel, an imported wine was used for the incense. Much more to the point is that "*kafrisin*" is the *modern* Hebrew name for the island of Cyprus, but is not found in ancient sources! And Rashi maintains that "*kafrisin* wine" is actually "*kapparis* wine," i.e., caper wine, and the *azzut*, the punging of the caper, rendered the *onycha* which was steeped in it *azzah*, pungent.

The remarkable fecundity of the caper is referred to on more than one occasion. It has even found its way into the *Halakhah*. Normally *ḥazakah* (presumption of ownership to property) is established by the presumptive owner gathering the crop of a field for three successive years without objection. The Talmud (*Bava Batra* 28b) asks whether the gathering of the crop of capers on three successive *days* would similarly establish presumptive ownership. It is also the basis of an incident related in the Talmud (*Shabbat* 30b). Rabban Gamaliel expounded that the time would come when fruit trees would yield their fruit every day. A certain disciple scoffed at the remark, quoting "there is nothing new under the sun." Rabban Gamaliel answered him, "Come, I will show you that this phenomenon exists today"—and showed him a caper bush.

The vicious thorns of the caper and its rapid spread made it eminently suitable as a protective hedge, and thereby hangs a tale in the Midrash. "It happened that a saintly man took a walk in his vineyard on the Sabbath and noticed that there was a breach in the hedge surrounding it and the thought came into his mind that he would have to repair it. But then he said to himself, 'I shall not do it, since I profaned the Sabbath by merely thinking about doing a manual task.' What did the Blessed Holy One do? He saw to it that a caper-bush should take root in the gap and it served as a hedge, and he had a livelihood from it for the rest of his life" (*Leviticus Rabbah* 34, end).

The first part of this last sentence is perfectly comprehensible since, as stated, the caper seed takes root and flourishes in any and every place along the roadside, in nooks and crannies in the wall, or on roofs of houses, and its vicious thorns make it an admirable hedge; but that it should be a source of economic livelihood "for the rest of one's life" is difficult to understand. (A few years ago a manufacturer of capers in Jerusalem used to give youngsters two *lira* for a kilogram of the buds. My own experience is that that represents about 2,000 buds. In few things is the spiralling inflation more evident than in the fact that he now has to pay IL. 40.00!) The answer, however, appears to me to be quite simple. The "it" in this sentence is not the caper, but the vineyard. The caper-bush acted as an effective protective hedge and ensured that the vineyard would not be ruined by trespassers.

I conclude by returning to the suggestion first made by Ephraim Ha-Reuveni that the biblical name Zelaphhad means "a sharp caper." Ha-Reuveni's son, Nogah, follows in his father's footsteps in his passion for the botany of Israel, and in a letter to me he advances an intriguing suggestion which can be termed "a Midrash on a Midrash."

When the daughters of Zelaphhad made their claim to inherit their father, they emphasized that although he had died in the wilderness, he had not been involved in the rebellion of Korah against Moses, but "he died as a result of his own sin" (Numbers 27:3). In the Talmud (*Shabbat* 96) Rabbi Akiva explains that he was the anonymous man who was put to death for gathering wood on the Sabbath (Numbers 15:32).

And Nogah Ha-Reuveni actually finds a connection between this identification and the name Zelaphhad. The caper grows in the driest and rockiest parts of the wilderness. Unlike most other shrubs, it flourishes in the summer, and when winter comes, whereas all other wood, whether of trees or of shrubs, is green and too damp to use as fuel, the twigs of the caper are bone dry, and to this day they constitute the main source of fuel for the Bedouin in winter. It was this characteristic which Rabbi Akiva had in mind when he identified the gatherer of the twigs on the Sabbath with Zelaphhad and, according to him, it was a name given to him because he had committed this sin. He was "the man of the sharp caper."

the CAROB

DEVARIM. DEUTERONOMY 1:1–3:22.
                    ISAIAH 1:1–27 (Haftarah)

> But if ye refuse and rebel, ye shall be devoured by
> the sword.   ISAIAH 1:20

"Everything depends upon *mazzal* [luck], even the *Sefer Torah*
in the ark" is a popular Hebrew proverb, which is often wrongly
ascribed to the Talmud, and the student of biblical flora can
add, "even the mention of flora in the Bible." The trees mentioned
in the Bible do not necessarily include all those trees which grew
in the Land of Israel during the biblical period. The number
of hapax legomena of trees which are mentioned only once
is unusually large; they include the walnut, the peanut and the
pine (*oren*, if it is indeed the pine), and their inclusion in the
Bible is almost accidental. There must have been some which
for some reason or other did not qualify for inclusion, and among
them, as Professor Judah Feliks points out, the carob is undoubtedly one. It is indigenous to the Land of Israel; it figures prominently both in fact and in legend in the Talmud; it is nowhere
referred to explicitly in the Bible, although Ibn Ezra maintains
that the *gerah* mentioned in Exodus 30:13 as the 20th part of
a shekel in weight, is the carob seed. It is, as Feliks points out,
probably the desire to fill this strange lacuna which is behind
the various attempts by medieval and modern scholars to identify
trees which are mentioned in Bible with it. Some modern
scholars, for instance, identify it with the *tirzah* of Isaiah 44:14.
Saadiah Gaon and Ibn Janah identify it with the *nekhot* mentioned
in the patriarchal narratives (Genesis 37:25), which would
make it one of the delicacies carried by caravan to Egypt.

Among modern attempts to identify it may be mentioned the
suggestion that the peculiar word *hiryonim* in II Kings 6:25

should be amended to read "*haruvim*," "carobs," a suggestion which has much to commend it.

The most remarkable attempt, however, to find mention of the carob in the Bible belongs to the most recent biblical scholarship, and it can be said of it "thereby hangs a tale," if the word Midrash can be loosely translated as "a tale."

For the rabbis apparently also felt the need to find a reference, even if a homiletical one, to the carob in the Bible, and they find it in a verse from the *Haftarah* of this Sabbath. In it the prophet describes the benefits which will accrue to the Children of Israel if they will but hearken to the word of the Lord, and the dire consequences of their failure to do so: "If ye be willing and obedient, ye shall eat of the good of the land." That verse, however, is followed by the obverse picture, "But if ye refuse and rebel, ye shall be devoured by the sword."

Thus, apparently, the opposite of "eating of the good of the land" is being "devoured by the sword." The rabbis of the Midrash, however, give an alternative homiletical translation, which on the face of it seems to border on the fantastic. Basing themselves on the fact that the biblical text is not vocalized, and that the letters of the word translated "ye shall eat" are identical with those for the word rendered "ye shall be devoured," instead of rendering it "ye shall be devoured by the sword," they render it—"ye shall eat carobs"!—the letters for the words "sword" and "carob" being identical.

Far-fetched though it may sound, it certainly produces a balanced verse: If ye will be willing and obedient, ye shall eat the good of the land, But if ye refuse and rebel, ye shall eat carobs!

The rabbis would have been the first to admit that this interpretation is no more than a homiletical *jeu d'esprit*, a *derash*, which is in contrast to the literal meaning, the *peshat*, and is employed only for homiletical purposes.

Judge therefore my astonishment when I saw that the sober and scientific (and sometimes pedestrian) translator of the New English Bible accepts this Midrashic near-pun as the literal meaning of the verse, and renders it: "But if you refuse and rebel, locust beans shall be your food!"

It does not entirely reject the translation "you shall be devoured by the sword" but relegates it to a footnote which it introduces with the awkward phrase, "or, with Scroll" (i.e., according to the Masoretic reading), but it is interesting that this translation which purports to be the fruit of 20 years of toil by the outstanding biblical scholars of the Protestant Church should accept this interpretation which the rabbis put forward as a mere intellectual play on words.

The carob thus emerges as the lowliest and most despised of foods, and so in fact it is represented both in the Talmud and the New Testament. In the Talmud it is stated of Rabbi Ḥanina ben Dosa, the miracle-working rabbi, that the Holy One, blessed be He, said of him, "The whole world is sustained by Ḥanina my son, yet he subsists on one *kab* of carobs from one eve of the Sabbath to the next." Of John the Baptist it is related that he lived in the desert on honey and "locusts." The word is generally taken to refer to the grasshoppers of that name, the name "St. John's bread" given to the carob pods in America, and "*Johannisbrot*" in German is due to the identification of the locusts of John with this fruit.

That the carob is the poor man's food which grows wild, and can be had merely for the picking, is made the basis of another Midrash the purpose of which is to give expression to the passionate and enduring love of the Jewish people for the Land of Israel, and their readiness to give up all material comforts and live in penury in exchange for that boon. The 84th Psalm refers to the longing of the Psalmist to dwell in the Temple. The word *histofef*, which is translated as "acting as a doorkeeper" (from "*saf*," a threshold) is, for this purpose, regarded as connected with a talmudic word, *sifufim*, which means the offal, the discarded ends of the carob pods, and David is made to say "I prefer to dwell in the Land of Israel even if my only sustenance is this carob offal, than enjoy affluence outside Israel."

Three names for the carob have already been mentioned: carob, locust and St. John's bread. At least two other names can be added, *panis graecis* ("Greek bread") and the Yiddish name *bokser*. This name is none other than a corruption of the German

Bockshorn, ram's horn, and the appearance of the curved brown pods is certainly suggestive of one. A special interest, however, attaches to the name carob. As stated above, Ibn Ezra, who is followed by most commentators, states that the *gerah* is none other than the carob seed. And so, originally, was the carat.

Despite the assonance of the two words carob and carat, however, there is apparently no semantic connection between them. The word 'carat' is derived from the Arabic *kirat*, which in its turn is derived from the Greek *keration*, meaning a little horn, referring to the carob pods (i.e., the exact equivalent of the German *Bockshorn* from which *bokser* is derived). According to the *Encyclopaedia Britannica* the carat is "a small weight, originally in the form of a seed, used for diamonds and precious stones, and a measure for determining the fineness of gold."

It is possible that this last definition of the carat may disappear from usage. In *The Times* of January 14, 1969, there appeared a news item to the effect that the Consumer's Council had asked the Board of Trade to abolish the carat system of marking gold. According to that report the carat system is widely misunderstood, and the public "tends to think it indicates varying quantities of gold." It goes on to explain that "a carat is actually a measure of the proportion of gold present, with a ceiling of 22 carats out of 24." Thus "nine-carat gold" means only 9/24 or 3/8 of gold, and 5/8 of base metal. "Gold alloy" might be a more accurate description. If this suggestion is accepted it will mean that to this extent the long life of the carob seed as the basis of a measurement, a life of some 3,500 years, will at last come to an end. But even if it is accepted, the life of the carat-carob will still continue as a measure for diamonds and precious stones.

That the carob was cultivated in mishnaic times is evident from the fact that according to the Mishnah (*Ma'aserot* 1:3) it is liable to tithes. It states that this liability commences "from the moment they become speckled." It is only when the fruit is completely ripe and fully brown without a green speck that it has its pleasant sweet taste; before that it has a peculiar astringent taste causing an unpleasant dessication of the gums and palate. An old Jew from Safed told me that there they apply to it in that stage the Russian name "*terbke*." Thus according to the Midrash *Lekah Tov* it is this quality which gives the Hebrew name *haruvim* to the tree since "it causes a drying of the teeth" (*harav*—to be dry). Other authorities also connect it with this root, but apply it to the fact that it grows in dry soil and does not need much water. Thus when Shakespeare refers to the "food that now to him is as luscious as locust shall be to him shortly as bitter as coloquintida" (Othello 1.3) he was referring to the poor quality of the fruit, the ripe pods.

The carob pods had a poor rating as regards their nutritional value, and the Talmud (*Sukkah* 53a) refers almost disparagingly to the poor quality of the fruit, the ripe pods. The context is interesting. It is universally accepted that the "fruit of the goodly tree" mentioned in Leviticus 23:40 is the *etrog*, the citron, but this identification depends entirely on the exegesis of the rabbis, and in the passage quoted they prove it by considering other alternatives and giving their reasons for rejecting them. After laying it down that the meaning of the words is that both the tree itself and the fruit are "goodly," they ask, "Perhaps it refers to the carob?" But they reject this possibility on the grounds that whereas the carob is indeed a "goodly tree," its fruit cannot be so regarded. The unkindest cut of all, however, comes from that great doctor and rabbinic authority, Maimonides. In a re-markable chapter in his *Mishneh Torah* in which he gives his health prescriptions, including diet and exercise, he reveals himself as having a poor opinion of fresh fruit generally in one's diet, but singles out carobs as being "always bad for health" (*Hilkhot De'ot*, 4:11).

Nevertheless, as one who is almost a carob addict (I provide myself with an annual supply of the juiciest pods I can find, and when they become dry, a mere soaking in water for 24 to 48 hours restores them to their pristine freshness), I can testify that the good quality carob pod has a delightful sweetness, and it is this characteristic which gives it another possible back-door entry into the Bible. Basing himself upon a statement by the medieval Arab philosopher Avicenna that the carob has the quality of rendering saline or brackish water sweet, a certain Sprengel suggests that the carob was the mysterious and anonymous tree which Moses cast into the bitter waters of Marah and thereby rendered them potable! (Exodus 15:25; see "The Desalinating Tree").

Thus does misfortune dog the carob, excluded from the flora of the Bible; regarded as the poor man's food; its nutritional qualities denigrated or denied. And that misfortune accompanies it to the present day. It was planted extensively in the Shephelah and elsewhere after the establishment of the State, with the aim of providing fodder for cattle, but it was found that the pods caused abortion in cows, and its use for this purpose had to be discontinued.

poor, learned tree!

VA-ETHANNAN. DEUTERONOMY 3:23–7:11.
                         ISAIAH 40:1–26 (Haftarah)

Ha-mesukkan terumah, *he chooseth a tree that will
not rot . . .*   ISAIAH 40:20

One of the most fascinating aspects of biblical exegesis lies in the
fact that one phrase is susceptible to more than one meaning, all
of which are possible and acceptable though there is not the
slightest connection between them. To give but two examples
which do not belong to the world of flora: the phrase *alufeinu
mesubbalim* in Psalm 144:4 is translated in the standard versions
as "our oxen are laden"; the Talmud takes it to mean "our
leaders are tolerated"! Similarly, the thousand "special" exiles
who were transported to Babylon with the first partial exile
under Jehoiachin in 597 B.C.E. (II Kings 23:16) are translated as
"craftsmen and locksmiths"; again the Talmud renders it as
"spiritual leaders and those who decided the law."

Examples in the world of flora are legion, and in fact many
words which are usually regarded as belonging to the world of
flora are regarded by others as appertaining to that of fauna. In
the previous chapter we have seen that the phrase translated
"You shall be devoured by the sword" is taken by some sober
scholars—apart from the rabbis of the Midrash—to mean "Ye
shall be reduced to eating carobs," and in the portion *Yitro* the
alternative translation to the oak tree "which casts its leaves" has
been given as "the oak tree which is by the Dung Gate," and the
reader will have noticed many others.

To the phrase discussed in this chapter, however, no less than
three different interpretations have been propounded, although
the general meaning is perfectly clear.

The *Haftarah* of this Sabbath, *Shabbat Nahamu*, contains a vivid
description of the fashioning of idols by idol worshipers. It
begins with a description of the manufacture of the graven image,

made of silver and plated with gold. It continues with the fashioning of the wooden idol, carved from a healthy tree trunk of
wood that will not rot. That description is preceded by the two
Hebrew words *ha-mesukkan terumah*, whose exact connotation
has exercised the minds of various commentators. That favored
by all the rabbinic commentators, with the exception of Rashi,
views the word *mesukkan* as a form of the well-known word
misken which in both Arabic and Hebrew means a poor man.
Terumah means an offering, and they therefore give the entirely
acceptable interpretation, which is adopted by the King James'
version, "He that is so impoverished that he hath no oblation."
The person who can afford it, fashions his idol out of precious
metal; the *misken* who cannot afford such an offering, has per-
force to satisfy himself with wood. He nevertheless chooses a
tree which will not be affected by the ravage of insects and hands
it to a skilled carpenter to make the idol. Thus, according to
this interpretation, *mesukkan* means 'poor.'

Rashi gives a strikingly different interpretation. He connects
the word with its use in Numbers 22:30 which, following the
Targum, he takes to mean in the active, "to learn." *Mesukkan*
therefore, means "learned"; *terumah* means "a choice," and he
thus explains the phrase to mean, "He who is expert in selection."
His expertise causes him to reject unsatisfactory wood which is
likely to rot and he selects that which is durable. And so, according
to Rashi, *mesukkan* means "learned."

The third explanation actually regards *mesukkan* as the name
of a tree, and thus renders the phrase, "when, however, his offering
is a *mesukkan* tree [and not an idol made of gold or silver], the
person who makes the offering takes care to choose a healthy
specimen which has not been attacked by insects and is not likely
to rot." The earliest authority I have found for this strange
explanation is the Targum, which renders it "a healthy pine."
In this identification of the *mesukkan* with a tree the Targum is
by no means unique, and the explanation has been accepted by
modern commentators and translators. The Jewish Publication
Society translation of the Bible renders it a "holm oak"; the
Soncino commentary comments, "others render it a palm tree

or a laurel"; while Segal, in his popular commentary, simply explains that *mesukkan* is a species of tree.

The New English Bible, however, which was mentioned in the previous chapter, identifies the *mesukkan*, on the basis of a root in Akkadian, with the mulberry tree. In fact, in the Authorized Version of the Bible, as well as in the translation of the Jewish Publication Society, the mulberry tree is mentioned, both of them so translating the *baca* tree mentioned in II Samuel 5:23. There is, to my mind, not the slightest justification for this rendering. The tree referred to is a rustling one. The New English Bible renders it the aspen, which is much more possible. But where it eliminates the mulberry as it appears in these versions, it makes up for it by identifying it with the *mesukkan*.

And combining these three proffered interpretations, all one can say is: Poor, learned tree!

honey

EKEV. DEUTERONOMY 7:12–11:25.

. . . A land of olive-trees and honey.

DEUTERONOMY 8:8

This week's portion includes an enumeration of the Seven Species, the agricultural products which the Talmud calls, literally, "the seven species for which the Land of Israel is praised," and which I always render, "which are the glory of the Land of Israel." They consist of two species of grain, wheat and barley, and five fruits, in that order: the vine, the fig, the pomegranate, the olive (particularly its oil), and the date.

All of these products have already been discussed, some at considerable length, but a special interest attaches to the last of them. The date palm is not mentioned in the verse specifically; the word used is *devash*, which has become proverbial in the oft-repeated (19 times in the Pentateuch) description of the Land of Israel as "a land flowing with milk and honey," a phrase which has already been discussed (see "Milk and Honey"). Now *devash* is, in fact, honey, but although it includes the juicy extract of the date, it is by no means confined to this, as will be explained. Yet the rabbis are so definite that in this context it refers specifically to the extract from the date of the palm, that on the authority of this verse they lay it down as a halakhic fact, to the extent that they include the date as one of the seven species from which alone the first fruits could be brought on the Festival of Pentecost (Deuteronomy 26:1–11).

At the present day we limit the word honey to bee honey, and not to an extract from the world of flora. Interestingly enough, the rabbis also apply the word *devash* to bee honey, though there is only one clear and explicit reference to bee honey in the Bible, in the famous riddle of Samson which derived from the incident of his seeing "a swarm of bees and honey in the carcass of the lion" (Judges 14) and because of the mention of *devash* as edible in the Bible, bee honey was permitted, despite a possible halakhic difficulty. Since it is a rule that "that which derives from an unclean animal is unclean," the honey which comes from an insect should be forbidden. However, they explain that the honey "is stored up in their bodies by the bees [from the pollen of plants] but is not an actual extract of the body of the bee." (See the whole interesting discussion in *Bekhorot* 7a.)

Thus while in the biblical period *devash* was essentially the juice exuding or extracted from fruit, not necessarily from dates (cf. Rashi to Leviticus 2:11 and to Song of Songs 5:1 where he actually applies the word to the juice extracted from sugar cane), it was primarily the juice of dates, although bee honey is also included.

During the period of the Mishnah, however, a complete transformation took place.

We have clear and incontrovertible evidence that during the talmudic period date honey was ousted by bee honey to such an extent that the Mishnah lays it down that, since in vowing, it is the meaning of the word as understood by the man in the street and not the literary meaning of the word which is decisive, if a man takes a vow to abstain from honey he is permitted to eat date honey (*Nedarim* 6:8), since by that time the word was identified with bee honey only.

But there is other evidence, and it is not without its amusing side, that during this period it was Babylon in which dates were plentiful, as has remained the case to this day. A Palestinian *amora*, Ulla, paid a visit to Babylon, and he was so impressed by the cheapness and superabundance of dates that he actually delivered himself of the opinion that the reason for the exile of the Jews to Babylon was that, finding dates so plentiful, they could devote themselves to the study of the Torah without economic worries. That bald statement is followed by an actual incident. Ulla inquired about the price of dates in the market and was told that they were at the ridiculously cheap price of three baskets, or one hamper, for a *zuz*. "What!" he said, "A hamper of dates for a *zuz*, and yet the Jews of Babylon do not devote themselves to the study of Torah?" But alas, he ate of them not too wisely but too well, and as a result of his over-indulgence he was seized with severe stomach cramps. He thereupon amended his previous statement, "What!" he said, "A hamper full of sharp knives [the parallel passage in *Ta'anit* 9b has 'a hamper full of deadly poison'] and yet the Babylonians can devote themselves to the study of Torah?" (*Pesaḥim* 87b, 88a).

A footnote with regard to an interpretation of the seven species is appended.

In a passage of the Talmud (*Berakhot* 41a) a certain Rabbi Hanan gives a remarkable and original interpretation of this verse and its enumeration. He maintained that the purpose of the verse is not to sing the agricultural praises of Israel but to give a list of the various standards of measurement of what is permitted and prohibited by Jewish ritual law, and ingeniously proceeds to indicate how each and every one of these species constitutes a standard of measurement, whether a barley corn, the size of a fig, an olive or a date, or the others.

The Talmud itself, in the ensuing discussion, points out that this interpretation is not to be taken literally since all these standards are of rabbinic, and not biblical, provenance, and this *tour de force* of Rabbi Hanan is to be regarded merely as a mnemonic, or an *asmakhta*—a supporting statement.

That very fact, however, is in itself an indication of the extent to which almost everything was, so to speak, measured by the rabbis by agricultural standards. True, there is the biblical *amah*, the cubit, originally the average length of the arm from the elbow to the wrist, as the English "foot" was originally the average length of a man's foot. There is one measurement which belongs to the world of fauna, the egg. But, overwhelmingly, as the reconstruction of Rabbi Hanan shows, it was to the world of flora that the rabbis turned to establish their standards of measurement.

pROVISION Of fOOD

RE'EH. DEUTERONOMY 11:26–16:17.

> *Then shalt thou turn it into money . . . and shalt go
> unto the place which the Lord thy God shall choose.
> And thou shalt bestow the money for whatever thy
> soul desireth . . .* DEUTERONOMY 14:25–26

The portion of this week gives the law of the *Ma'aser Sheni*,
the Second Tithe, which, unlike the First Tithe which was given
to the Levite, was retained by the farmer and eaten by him when
he came on pilgrimage to Jerusalem on the three Pilgrim Festivals.
That pilgrimage was not for physical recreation, but for spiritual
re-creation. If one rejoiced, it was "a rejoicing before the Lord";
if one "went to a show," it was "to 'show' oneself before the
Lord."

That concentration on the spiritual aspect of these pilgrimages
is the subject of a lovely homily in the Talmud, which makes a
positive virtue of the comparative agricultural barrenness of the
hill country around Jerusalem, as compared with the fecund
fertility of the area of the Kinneret: "Why do not the luscious
fruits of Ginnosar grow in the vicinity of Jerusalem? In order
that it should not be said that the purpose of the pilgrimage was
to indulge one's physical appetites."

These appetites had nevertheless to be satisfied. Does not the
passage specifically state "And ye shall eat before the Lord, in
the place where he shall choose His name to dwell"? And in view
of the paucity of local supplies, whence was that food to come?
The verse continues, "the tithe of the corn, thine oil and thy
wine." And so the pilgrim brought his own supplies of food,
from his own bountiful harvest.

But these were the days before cold storage and refrigeration,
and other modern technological advances which make it possible
to preserve food. Nor could he bring large supplies of preserved
fruits such as raisins and other dried fruits, since the tithe had

to be from the produce of that self-same year. What, then, was the pilgrim from distant parts to do? By the time he reached the Capital and the Temple, his fruit would have gone bad. And wisely, the Bible makes specific provision for this contingency. "In the event that the way is too far for you," then it was laid down that the pilgrim was permitted to sell his produce in his own locality and bring monetary proceeds with him to Jerusalem. And there he could spend it freely—but, according to the Talmud, only on such things as grew from the earth, whether directly in the form of flora, or indirectly in that of fauna.

trees in Jerusalem

SHOFETIM. DEUTERONOMY 16:18–21:9.

Thou shalt not plant a grove of any trees near unto the altar of the Lord . . . DEUTERONOMY 16:21

It was a routine meeting of the Jerusalem Municipal Council, which was to all intents and purposes a rubber-stamping of the reports of the various committees. Among them was one giving the regulations with regard to the responsibilities of fortunate owners of homes in the Old City. One of these was the requirement to plant trees, shrubs and so on, as and when requested to do so by the Municipality.

To this clause a representative of the Agudat Yisrael political party objected strongly. "One cannot oblige a person to do something which is a breach of the *Halakhah*," he maintained, pointing out that according to the Talmud, one of the things forbidden in Jerusalem was the planting of trees.

In point of fact we are specifically informed by the Talmud that during the time of the Second Temple, among the special ten municipal regulations applying to Jerusalem was one to the effect that "neither gardens nor orchards should be cultivated there, with the exception of the rose garden which existed there from the days of the early prophets" (*Bava Kamma* 82b). The rose garden was almost certainly the "king's garden" mentioned in the Bible, which was in the area of the Pool of Siloam; where this passage limits the prohibition to "gardens and orchards," the parallel passages (*Tosefta, Negaim* 6:2; *Avot de-Rabbi Nathan* 35) specifically include all trees and plantings in the prohibition.

But before we pass censure on the authorities of the city for maintaining such a "municipal by-law," which would appear to condemn them as lacking in aesthetic appreciation, it must be mentioned that the reason given for this strange prohibition is that it was instituted in order to *improve* the amenities of the capital! The reason proffered is "on account of the bad odor."

To that offense against the olfactory senses Rashi adds: "And in order to keep Jerusalem clean. It was because of the profusion of weeds which they would throw into the thoroughfare, as well as on account of the offensive smell given off by the manure which they were accustomed to use."

Be that as it may, there seems to be little doubt that to the extent that this prohibition was put into effect, it was an extension of a prohibition which occurs in this week's portion. The verse under discussion in this chapter is understood by the rabbis to mean, "Thou shalt not plant an *asherah* [a sacred grove used in Canaanite worship] or any tree near the altar of the Lord." From this interpretation is derived the prohibition that "whosoever plants a tree in the area of the Temple Mount transgresses a negative commandment."

The only authority among the medieval codifiers who includes this prohibition in his Code is Maimonides, who lays it down (*Hilkhot Avodah Zarah* 6:9): "He who plants a tree next to the altar, or indeed anywhere within the area of the Temple court-yard, whether it be a fruitbearing tree or not, even if his intention was solely in order to beautify the Sanctuary, is guilty of a transgression" (see also *Hilkhot Beit ha-Beḥirah* 7:14). He gives as the reason for this prohibition that it was the custom of idol-worshipers to plant groves of trees around their sacred places as an added inducement of attraction for people to assemble there. The implication is that ancillary attractions to the pure worship of God were to be frowned upon, and much could be written of Maimonides' consistency in this view, and the objection on the part of the Agudah members of the municipality was based upon this codification of the law.

It should be pointed out, however, that—in line with Maimonides' inference—Prof. S. Krauss expressed the opinion that the prohibition applied only to the Temple Mount.

However, as even those persons who heed the prohibition of the Chief Rabbinate against entering the precincts of the Temple Mount—a prohibition which to my mind does not apply to the southern extension on which stands the El Aksa mosque—can still see from Mt. of Olives on the east, and from the roofs of the houses in the Jewish quarter of the Old City to the west, there is a not inconsiderable number of majestic trees on the Temple Mount which add to its beauty.

It seems that this feature of trees in the courtyard of the Temple was equally characteristic of the Temple of Solomon. The most acceptable rendering of the verse in the Sabbath Psalm (92:12–13), "The righteous shall flourish like the palm tree and grow like the Cedar of Lebanon, which are planted in the House of the Lord, which shall continue to flourish in the courts of our Lord," is to my mind that it is the trees which are planted, and not the righteous! There is also reason to believe that even during the period of the Second Temple the prohibition was disregarded, or, as suggested by Prof. Krauss, strictly limited to the Temple area alone.

The Old City as a whole does not lack trees today. They are especially prominent on the Temple Mount and in the Armenian Quarter. Many in the latter area have, alas, been cut down to make way for the new Armenian seminary. There is a reasonable tradition that these are the descendants of trees which, in defiance of the prohibition, or prior to it, the Hasmonean and Herodian rulers planted around their palace. This stretched from where the old "Kishle" prison and police station now stands to the site of the seminary. In glaring contrast to this prohibition in the time of the Second Temple was a large placard recently prominently displayed on the municipal notice boards of Jerusalem, calling attention to the fact that the cutting down of trees without permission was a criminal offense, involving stringent penalties, and it actually appealed, *mirabile dictu*, to all citizens to inform the police or the municipal authorities of any instances of such vandalism so that appropriate action could be taken.

leket, shikhhah and pe'ah

KI TEZE. DEUTERONOMY 21:10–25:19.

> *When thou reapest thy harvest in thy field, and has forgot a sheaf in the field, thou shalt not go back to fetch it . . . When thou beatest thine olive-tree, thou shalt not go over the bough again . . .*
>
> DEUTERONOMY 24:19–20

I have been privileged to become a kind of honorary member of a kibbutz not far from Jerusalem, and that membership carries with it a valuable privilege of which I am able to take full advantage. It is of helping myself to the fruit which has remained in their extensive orchards after the harvest has been gathered. No matter how thoroughly that harvesting has been performed, there is always some fruit left on the trees, and from July to September I have been able to help myself freely to luscious peaches, splendid apples, and juicy plums which otherwise would have been left simply to rot on the trees.

That privilege is one of three, *leket, shikhhah,* and *pe'ah,* which are three different aspects of the same heart-warming biblical injunction that the farmer is enjoined to leave a portion of his produce for the use of the stranger, the fatherless and the poor and indigent. The *leket* is the "gleanings," the individual grapes as distinct from the whole clusters, the single olives left on the branch, etc. *Shikhhah,* according to the literal meaning of the Bible, is the sheaf of corn which the harvester left behind in his field, through forgetfulness, but which the rabbis extend to every produce so left, while *pe'ah* is the corner of the field, the extent of which was left entirely to the generosity of the farmer. Legally, he could fulfill the letter of the law by leaving one stalk, but the rabbis suggested from between one-fortieth and one-sixtieth of his crop.

As the person who has even only a nodding acquaintance with rabbinic literature knows, the three words *leket*, *shikhḥah*, and *pe'ah* are always mentioned together, although nowhere in the Bible are all three mentioned in one passage. In the portion of this week *shikhḥah* and *leket* are enjoined, while in Leviticus 19:9 and 23:22 *pe'ah* and *leket* are referred to.

There is surely no need to seek any special ethical lesson to be derived from these humane laws, enacted at a time when consideration for the poor and unfortunate was regarded as the duty of every individual instead of, as today, the responsibility of the state. But once that provision for the poor has become an integral part of the modern welfare state and the poor person is no longer expected to rely upon private charity, it might be thought that they have no relevance today. The rabbis, however, are never satisfied with the patent, obvious moral enshrined in the injunctions of the Bible and always seek to deduce other and more profound moral lessons than the obvious ones. Two examples of these lessons derived from the laws of *leket*, *shikhḥah*, and *pe'ah* merit mention.

A moment's consideration will bring the realization that there is a conspicuous difference between *pe'ah* and *leket* on the one hand, and *shikhḥah* on the other. *Pe'ah* and *leket* have to be left as a deliberate conscious act of consideration on the part of the farmer, whereas the *shikhḥah* is the result of forgetfulness. Had the farmer remembered it he would not have left it! And there would be no *mitzvah*.

This point is lovingly seized upon by the rabbis to press home a moral both in the form of an interpretation and a lovely story. The interpretation (briefly quoted by Rashi) is in the *Sifre* to Leviticus 5:19 in the name of Rabbi Eleazar ben Azariah: "The Torah promises a blessing to the person who happens to fulfill a *mitzvah* without any conscious act on his part. From this one can deduce the truth that if a man had a coin bound up in the corner of his garment and it fell out, and a poor man found it and benefited from it, a blessing accrues to the owner of that coin, since it is like *shikhhah* in the field." And the point is illustrated by the moving story told in the *Tosefta* (*Pe'ah* 3:8): "It happened that a certain pious man forgot a sheaf in his field. When he realized it he said to his son, 'Go and offer up a sacrifice of thanksgiving and a peace-offering on my behalf.' Said his son to him, 'Why do you rejoice with this *mitzvah* more than with any other *mitzvah* of the Torah?' And he replied, 'All other *mitzvot* come as the result of the conscious act of the performer, save for this one. This one accrues as a result of forgetfulness. If therefore a blessing is promised for a *mitzvah* which is performed without intention, how much greater is the reward of him who performs one with full intention.'" No less heartwarming is the lesson derived by the rabbis from the fact that the injunction to fulfill the laws of *leket* and *pe'ah* comes in an unusual context in Leviticus 23:22, and it served to arouse the intellectual and spiritual curiosity of the rabbis. With the exception of this law the chapter deals exclusively with an enumeration of the five biblical Festivals, the three Pilgrim Festivals and Rosh Ha-Shanah and Yom Kippur, detailing the various sacrifices which had to be offered up in the Temple during them. And it is there, sandwiched in between the regulations of the Festivals of Shavuot and Rosh Ha-Shanah, that there comes the interruption of these laws of charity and concern for the poor. Said Rabbi Avdimi, the son of Rabbi Jose, "For what reason did the Torah see fit to insert these laws between Passover and Shavuot on one hand, and Rosh Ha-Shanah and Yom Kippur on the other? To teach thee that whosoever gives *leket*, *shikhhah*, and *pe'ah* to the poor is regarded as though he had built the Temple and offered up in it the requisite sacrifices."

spices

. . . They shall bring gold and frankincense . . .

ISAIAH 60:6

The *Haftarah* of this Sabbath is the sixth of the seven "*haftarot* of consolation" read from the Sabbath after Tishah be-Av until the Sabbath before Rosh Ha-Shanah. All of them are from the latter half of the Book of Isaiah, and all foretell the imminent Return to Zion and the restoration of the Jewish State after the Babylonian Exile.

The *Haftarah* of this Sabbath presages a state of affairs of which there has been little evidence in the emergence of the modern State of Israel; the nations of the world, in appreciation of that miracle, pouring their wealth into the country in order to rehabilitate it, and even taking an active part in its upbuilding.

Among these countries is mentioned Sheba, and the wealth which it will contribute is referred to as "gold and *levonah* [frankincense]."

This *levonah*, which was one of the ingredients of the holy incense used in the Temple (Exodus 30:34), is to be taken in the context as referring to spices generally, and the juxtaposition of the two words—gold, the most precious metal known in ancient times, and spices—is a clear indication of the immense value of spices in ancient as in medieval, times. When, in 408 C.E., Alaric the Hun sacked Rome, he demanded inter alia, 3,000 lbs. of pepper as part of the ransom, and it is a historical fact that the stimulus for the Portuguese explorers to seek a sea route to India was to cash in on this lucrative trade. In fact, the drop in prices came only with that discovery. The verse of our text is not the only occasion when gold is coupled with spices. Among the gifts which the Queen of Sheba brought to King Solomon were—in that order—"spices, and very much gold, and precious stones" (I Kings 10:2).

When Berodach Baladan, King of Babylon, sent a delegation to King Hezekiah to congratulate him on his recovery from an illness, to the subsequent consternation and dismay of the prophet Isaiah he opened up to the view of the members of this diplomatic mission all the contents of his treasury, which are enumerated as "silver, gold, spices and the precious ointment" (II Kings 20:13; Isaiah 39:2), and the interesting fact is that this treasure house was named, not after the silver and gold which were stored up in it, but after the spices. It is called *Bet Nechot*, and *nechot* is the name of a famous spice (cf. Genesis 37:25 and 43:11).

The reason for this immense value of spices is of course that they all came from the Far East, and Prof. J. Feliks, the biblical and talmudic botanist, is at pains to maintain that the garden of spices mentioned in Song of Songs 4:14, the most detailed list of spices and fragrant perfumes mentioned in the Bible, is an imaginary garden, in striking contrast to the rest of the wealth of flora mentioned in that book, since few, if any, of these spices grew in the Land of Israel.

The rabbis were naturally equally aware of this apparent anomaly, but they explain it differently. They make Solomon, the traditional author of Song of Songs, an expert gardener— did he not "speak of trees, from the cedar that is in Lebanon unto the hyssop that springeth out of the wall?" (I Kings 5:33), a phrase which implies the whole gamut of the world of flora (and of Ecclesiastes 2:4–6, which is also traditionally ascribed to Solomon), and they comment: "Solomon knew and traced the veins of soil which led from the Land of Israel to the Far East, and on them he planted the seeds of the precious spices."

gall and wormwood

NIẒẒAVIM. DEUTERONOMY 29:9–30:20.

. . . Lest there should be among you a root that beareth gall and wormwood . . . DEUTERONOMY 29:17

Rosh and *la'anah*, translated "gall and wormwood," are the traditional bitter, if not even poisonous, herbs in the Bible. They first occur together in this week's portion. In his concluding address to his people before he bids them his last farewell, Moses, the Faithful Shepherd, warns them against turning away from God to serve other gods. Such a person is "a root bearing gall and wormwood," the phrase obviously implying the harboring of evil and unworthy thoughts. Both the combination *rosh vela'anah* and word *la'anah* itself are used in other senses in the Bible, but all of them, without exception, are in pejorative ones. In Proverbs 5:3–4 we read of the strange woman "whose lips drop honeycomb and her mouth is smoother than oil, but her end is bitter as wormwood," while in Amos 5:7 the prophet inveighs against those who "turn justice to wormwood and leave off righteousness in the earth," and the author of Lamentations cries out, "Remember my affliction and misery, gall and wormwood" (3:19).

The word "wormwood" is in itself interesting. It has nothing to do with wood which has been attacked and rotted by insects. It is a typical example of the tendency in English to change strange-sounding foreign words into similar-sounding homely English words. "Asparagus" becomes "sparrow grass" and the much more dignified word in the world of lexicography, "vermouth," becomes "wormwood."

For the *la'anah* is beyond any doubt a plant of the species *Artemisia* and of that species the *Artemisia absinthum* is the wormwood, or vermouth. There is, in the Talmud, a reference to wormwood of which I was completely unaware. The phrase "hard as *giddim*" occurs on various occasions in the homiletical literature of the rabbis. For instance the Talmud (*Shabbat* 87a) homiletically interprets the word *va-yaged* ("told") in the verse, "and Moses told the words of God to the Children of Israel," to the effect that "He told them words hard as *giddim*." The word was well known to me from my talmudic studies:

I knew of the most famous of all *giddim*, the *gid ha-nasheh*, "the sinew which shrank" as a result of Jacob's mysterious midnight struggle with the angel, and the consequent prohibition of eating that part of an animal. I still remember by heart the first Mishnah of the ninth chapter of *Hullin* which speaks of the "hide, the bones and the *giddim* of animals," which are, of course, also sinews and the halakhic statement that those *giddim* are tasteless and do not add any flavor to food with which they are cooked; and of course I knew that the thread with which the sheets of parchment of the *Sefer Torah* are sewn together and to the rollers should preferably be made of *giddim* which is, of course, the gut made from the sinews. In other words I had no doubt whatsoever that *giddim* belonged to the world of fauna, that it meant "tough and indigestible as the gristle, or the sinews, of meat," and had no connection whatsoever with the world of flora which is my sphere. But I was wrong. To my surprise, I found that all the commentators without exception maintain that *giddim*, where it is used as a simile for hardness, has nothing to do with sinews or the world of fauna, but belongs to the world of flora and refers to the proverbial wormwood. Without exception the word *la'anah* is rendered *giddim* in the Aramaic Targum to the Prophets (e.g., Jeremiah 9:4, 23:16; Amos 5:7). The most interesting proof of it, however, is to be found in a passage of the *Tanhuma* which deals with the manna.

Rabbi Jose ben Hanina states that this miraculous food had whatever taste the consumer of it found most delectable. To the children it tasted like milk, to the young men like honey, to the old people like bread, to invalids like fine flour mixed with milk and honey—each one found in it a taste according to his strength. That, however, applied only to the Children of Israel. "The nations of the world could not eat it, since it was as bitter as *giddim* to their palates. What did they do? They hunted a hind which had eaten it and, by eating its flesh, tasted the flavor of manna." And Rashi in his comment on our verse says simply, "a root which produces a plant as bitter as *giddim*, which are bitter."

As to the identity of the *rosh*, however, there is a difference of opinion. Despite the English rendering of the word as "gall," which is none other than the bitter bile of the gall bladder, most authorities agree, as is evident from the verse quoted above which speaks of a root bearing gall, that it is primarily a plant which produces a bitter extract ("the waters of *rosh*," Jeremiah 8:14; 9: 14, etc.), and that its use for other poisons, e.g., snake venom (Deuteronomy 32:33), is a secondary meaning.

The famous grammarian Gesenius, basing himself on the fact that the word is identical with the Hebrew word for "head" (only once, in Deuteronomy 32:33, is it spelt with a *vav* instead of an *alef*), identifies the plant with the poppy, and its extract with opium. I am inclined to regard that identification as a far-fetched one which belongs to the period before biblical botany became an exact science, and I personally prefer the identification with the colocynth. I was, however, interested to see that Prof. J. Feliks, although he agrees that the data given render its exact identification impossible, and gives three possible ones, prefers the identification of Gesenius, and in accordance with that regards the modern Hebrew word for the poppy, *pereg*, as a mistake.

The definition given by S. Mandelkern in his concordance of the Bible is of interest: he states that the *rosh* is a fragrant plant, but it came to be applied to poison, in the same way as the word *sam*, which is mentioned among the ingredients of the incense and was thus a fragrant plant, became confined in its meaning to one plant, the *sam ha-mavet*, "the plant of death," and as a result the word alone now means merely poison.

This chapter is such a "bitter" one that it is almost with relief that one finds that no less a figure than S. Y. Agnon turns *la'anah* from a source of bitterness to one of delight. *La'anah* is the source of absinthe, its basis being a dark green oil, known as "oil of wormwood," extracted from its leaves, and the following passage occurs in Agnon's novel *Hakhnassat Kallah*:

> When Paltiel heard that Reb Yudel was setting out on a journey for the purpose of fulfilling the sacred duty of *hakhnassat kallah* (dowering a bride), he brought out a bottle of *la'anah* brandy and cake, and they sat down by the fireplace.
>
> *La'anah* brandy is the choicest of liquors, and it is neither common nor widespread. Here is the recipe for its manufacture: The leaves of the *la'anah* are gathered and placed in a barrel of brandy. The barrel is kept sealed until the liquid turns as green as the leaves, while the leaves become saturated with brandy. Then the leaves are taken out and pressed, and the emerging liquid collected.
>
> But what is one to do before it is ready? Alas, he has to content himself with ordinary brandy.

wine of Lebanon

VA-YELEKH. DEUTERONOMY 31.
       HOSEA 14:2–10; MICAH 7:18–20; JOEL
       2:15–17 (Haftarah, Shabbat Shuvah)

. . . The scent thereof shall be as the wine of Lebanon.
HOSEA 14:8

Thrice in three successive verses is the Lebanon mentioned in the
last chapter of the prophet Hosea, which forms part of the
Haftarah of *Shabbat Shuvah*, the Sabbath between the solemn
festival of Rosh Ha-Shanah and the even more solemn Day of
Atonement. Verse 6 speaks of "casting his roots as Lebanon,"
probably a reference to the lofty and majestic cedar of Lebanon
which stretches its roots deep in the inhospitable rocky soil of
the mountain. The next verse speaks of the fragrant odor of the
Lebanon, while verse 8 refers to the fragrant wine of Lebanon.

This is the only reference in the Bible to the Lebanon as a
wine-growing area, and that a wine which apparently possessed
a distinctive, characteristic bouquet. According to one interpretation of a well-known passage of the Talmud, however, there
is a reference if not actually to the wine of Lebanon, at least to
the wine of that area, and the reference also suggests that it had
a particular pungency or fragrance.

A passage of the Talmud (*Keritot* 6a) which is included in the
prayer book where it is known by its opening words as *Pittom
ha-Ketoret* gives the various ingredients, and their quantities,
which make up the incense which was used in the Second Temple.
It includes the passage, of which the accepted translation is "of
Cyprus wine three *se'ah* and three *kab*," but, if Cyprus wine was
not available, old white wine could be substituted. It concluded
with the reason for the addition of this "Cyprus wine." "The
Cyprus wine was used to steep it [the *onycha*] in, so that its odor
might be pungent." As has already been pointed out in the chapter
on the caper, the correct translation of the phrase translated

153

"Cyprus wine" is almost certainly "caper wine," which, inter alia, explains the "pungency" which is characteristic of the caper. There are also those, however, who maintain that "old *havvaryon* wine" does not mean "old white wine" (*hivver* means "white" in Aramaic), but "wine of Hauran." The Hauran is a district in northeastern Transjordan, today part of Syria. It figures prominently in the history and the geography of the period of the Second Temple when it was part of the Jewish state and it was one of the places where beacons were kindled to announce the coming of the New Moon (*Rosh Ha-Shanah* 2:4), but it is mentioned in Ezekiel 47:16–17 where it is spelt *Havran*, of which *hivvaryon* is an acceptable adjective. The Hauran was adjacent to the Lebanon and the same species of grapes which grow in the one would have grown in the other. The Talmud passage tells us that, where no caper wine, with its pungency, was available, Hauran wine, according to this interpretation, could be substituted. Obviously then it had a particular pungency, and similarly "the Lebanon wine" of the prophet is singled out for its special bouquet of fragrance.

If this interpretation can be accepted, *kafrisin* wine ceases to indicate the provenance of the wine, while *hivvaryon* wine, its substitute, does!

vine of sodom

HA'AZINU. DEUTERONOMY 32.

> *For their vine is the vine of Sodom, and of the fields of Gomorrah, their grapes of gall, their wine is the poison of dragons.* DEUTERONOMY 32:32

In this week's portion, which is the wondrous poem of the future destiny of Israel delivered by Moses on the last day of his life, is mentioned "the vine of Sodom."

Most of the modern commentators regard the "vine of Sodom" as the name of a distinctive plant, though they differ in their identification of it. There are those who stress the word "vine" and therefore seek to identify it with a plant with trailing tendrils, the fruit of which, as the context implies, is bitter, and they therefore identify it with the plant picturesquely called in the Mishnah "*yerikat* [not *yerukat*] *ha-ḥamor*," "the spitting donkey," the *Ecbalium elaterium*. When its fruit, which look like small cucumbers, are ripe, a mere touch causes them to shoot off the stem, squirting their bitter juice. Alternatively it is identified with the colocynth (*Citrullus colocynthus*). Others stress the word Sodom, which would indicate that it grows specifically in the area of the Dead Sea, and they thus reject the above identification, since both these plants grow extensively throughout the whole country. They therefore identify it with the plant called today "the Sodom apple," the *Calotropis procera*, which the distinguished botanist Prof. Zohari identifies with the *petillat ha-midbar* mentioned in the second chapter of *Mishnah Shabbat* (*Ba-Meh Madlikim*), the fiber of which is not permitted for the wick of the Sabbath lamp since it forms an unsatisfactory wick. This apple of Sodom, as its name implies, grows extensively particularly in the Dead Sea area, and the beautiful shrub with its strange fruit can be seen as an ornamental plant in the garden of the modern hotel on the shores of the Dead Sea.

These apples of Sodom are mentioned by ancient writers such

as Strabo, Pliny, and Tacitus; and Josephus actually says of them
that they "have a color as if they were fit to be eaten but, if you
pluck them they dissolve into smoke and ashes." If the reference
is indeed to the apple of Sodom it is an exaggeration, though a
pardonable and understandable one; the fruit looks most in-
viting—it looks like a large apple or a quince—but insofar as
eating it is concerned, it can truly be said that it "dissolves like
smoke and ashes." Its soft skin is filled with a multitude of seeds
surrounded by long white silky strands, but there is no part of
it which is edible.

The rabbinic commentators, however, do not accept that the
name "vine of Sodom" refers to a specific plant, and they see a
significance in the fact that its twin town of evildoers, Gomorrah,
is mentioned together with it. To them "Sodom and Gomorrah"
have the same connotation here as is found everywhere else in
the Bible, as signifying something utterly corrupt and vicious.
Isaiah, for instance, refers to the corrupt leaders of Jerusalem of
his time as "rulers of Sodom, people of Gomorrah" (1:10). In
other words, the "vines of Sodom" are ordinary grapevines but
which have gone wild and produced clusters of bitter grapes.
And in Isaiah 5 we have his powerful metaphor of the Children
of Israel who have gone astray that "he hoped to produce choice
grapes but produced wild grapes." These would be the "vine of
Sodom."

It is this interpretation which provides the basis for one of
the identifications of the anonymous Tree of the Knowledge of
Good and Evil as the vine. Both in the Talmud (*Berakhot* 40a)
and in the Midrash (*Genesis Rabbah* 15:8) the identity of this
tree is discussed. Various suggestions are put forward, but the
most favored are the fig, which is the subject of the first chapter
of this volume, and the vine; the fig because it was with fig
leaves that Adam and Eve covered their nakedness and "with
that with which they went astray they were put right."

In the Talmud it is Rabbi Meir who propounds the view that
it was the vine, but he bases his suggestion upon the statement
that "it is the source of most lamentation and sorrow in the
world." In the Midrash it is Rabbi Judah who upholds this view;

but he supports it by quoting a proof verse from the Bible. And that verse is the verse of our text: "Their grapes are grapes of *rosh* and their clusters are bitter," since "it was those clusters which brought bitterness to the world."

fraudulent flora

. . . For they shall suck the abundance of the seas, and the hidden treasures of the sand.

DEUTERONOMY 33:19

The last portion of the Torah, *Ve-Zot he-Berakhah*, is the only portion which is not read on a Sabbath, but is reserved for the completion of the reading of the annual cycle on Simḥat Torah. In both the formal blessings of Jacob to his twelve sons (Genesis 49:13) and that of Moses to the Twelve Tribes descended from them (Deuteronomy 33:19) the blessing of Zebulun is connected with the fact that the inheritance of that tribe included the northern sea of the Land of Israel which, with the adjoining seashore, would be the source of its prosperity. Jacob's blessing is "Zebulun shall dwell at the shore of the sea, and it shall be a shore for ships and his flank shall be at Sidon," while Moses states of him, "They shall suck the abundance of the sea." In addition to the prosperity based upon fishing and shipping, however, there was in ancient times an added source of lucrative income from the sea by Zebulun—the fact that the immensely valuable *ḥillazon*, a mollusc from which the *tekhelet*, the blue dye which was used to make the ritual fringes, the *ẕiẕit* of the *tallit*, as well as the famed royal purple of the Romans, were from this area of the Mediterranean coast.

So far we are entirely in the world of fauna and not of flora. During the talmudic period, however, this, the early source of genuine dye permissible for this ritual use, became more and more rare until it was stated that this mollusc appeared only once in 70 years (*Menaḥot* 44a) and unscrupulous merchants used an illegal substitute obtained from a plant called *kala ilan*, probably indigo, and palmed off this fraudulent substitute on the pious. There was at that time no scientific method for detecting the fraud, and the rabbis therefore had to content themselves with

158

appealing to the people to acquire their *tekhelet* only from a reliable person (*Menaḥot* 42b), and in execrating in the most extreme terms the perpetrators of this fraud. "The Holy One, blessed be He, declared 'It is I who distinguished in Egypt between the firstborn and those not firstborn; even so it is I who will exact from him who . . . attaches to his garments threads dyed with *kala ilan* and claims that it is the true blue of *tekhelet*.'"

Modern scientific methods, however, make it possible to detect such a fraud, and as a result after over 1850 years it was possible to establish that this mean fraud was perpetrated on none other than the gallant soldiers of Bar Kokhba! In the caves of the Dead Sea where the Bar Kokhba letters were discovered, Prof. Yigael Yadin also found some dyed fringes. He submitted them for scientific analysis to Mr. Edelstein of the Dexter Chemical Corporation, the greatest expert on dyes in the world, who found that they had been dyed with indigo and not with *tekhelet*. Thus were the pious warriors of Bar Kokhba the victims of this fraudulent flora!

INDEXES

A. SCRIPTURAL REFERENCES
According to Chapter and Verse of Books of Bible.

GENESIS

1:11—26
2:5—10
3:7—1
3:17—26
3:21—76
6:12—4
8:11—3
12:6—5
18:8—7
21:15—10
21:23—11
21:33—7, 56
24:66—10
26:12—11
27:27—12
30:37—14
35:4—5
35:8—16
37:25—127, 148
38:6—18
41:2—21
41:42—70
43:11—148

45:23—23
46—56
48:16—103
49:11—25
49:13—158

EXODUS

3:1—120
3:2—27
3:8—32, 33
3:17—32, 33
7:21—103
9:25—85
9:31—71
9:31-32—30
13:5—32
15:25—35, 132
16:3—101
16:33—110
22:9—41
26:12—55
26:28—58
27:20—46
28:42—70

29:2—46
30:13—127
30:34—147
34-35—52
35:24—55, 57
39:24—61
39:28—70

LEVITICUS

1:7—64
2:11—137
5:1—99
5:19—145
6:3—70
6:12-13—64
13:47—76
14:4—78
18:3—81
19:9—145
23:10—87
23:15-16—87
23:22—145, 146
23:40—131
25:2—90

NUMBERS

3:6—96
4:29–37—59
5:15—87
6:3–4—98
11:5—14, 101
11:35—118
12:11—118
12:16—118
13:20—105
13:23—61
15:13—33
15:32—125
17:23—108
17:24—110
17:25—110
19:6—78, 111
19:19—110
20:5—61
22:30—134
24:5—79
24:6—67, 114
25—58
27:3—125
33—117
36:2—122

DEUTERONOMY

8:8—1, 37, 61,
    88, 107, 136
11:30—5
12:2—91
14:25–26—139
16:21—141
20:19—20
20:20—65
24:19–20—144
26:1–11—136
26:9—32
26:15—32
29:17—149
32:32—155

32:33—151
33:16—27
33:19—158
33:24—48

JOSHUA

2:6—30, 71
4:19—30

JUDGES

7:13—88
9—43
14—136

I SAMUEL

17:28—120

II SAMUEL

5:23—135
6:5—73

I KINGS

4:33—78
5:8—88
5:13—43
5:26—43
5:33—148
10:2—147
10:27—84
14:5—79
18:5—102
19:4—116

II KINGS

4:39—63
6:25—127
14:9—113

20:13—148
23:16—133
41:12—88

ISAIAH

1:8—101
1:10—156
1:20—127
5—156
6:13—39
7:22—34
39:2—148
40:20—133
41:19—74, 112
44:14—127
44:16—21
60:6—147
60:13—74
61:9—82

JEREMIAH

1:11—15, 108
2:2—119
2:6—119
8:14—151
9:4—150
9:14—151
11:6—47
17:6—93
17:8—93
23:16—150
36:22—21

EZEKIEL

27:5—73
27:6—74
27:16—71
47:16–17—154

HOSEA

13:15—21
14:6–8—153

AMOS

5:7—149, 150
7:14–15—84

MICAH

4:3—1

PSALMS

9:12—113
25:15—82
78:47—85
84—129
92—80
92:12–13—143
92:13—89, 96
98:7—89
102—89
102:18—94
104—102

120:4—116, 117
128—50
144:4—133
148—89, 111
148:1, 9—44

PROVERBS

5:3–4—149
7:23—63
31:19—76

JOB

8:11—21
14:7–9—9
30:4—117

SONG OF SONGS

2:12—81
4:3—63
4:11—32
4:14—148
5:1—137
6:11—67, 114
7:9—12
8:2—63

LAMENTATIONS

3:19—149

ECCLESIASTES

2:4–6—148
12:5—15, 123

ESTHER

1:6—77

EZRA

2:52—103

NEHEMIAH

2:13—40
3:14—40
10:35—64
12:31—40

I CHRONICLES

13:8—74
26:16—40

B. FLORA

English, Latin and Hebrew Names

A

Acacia 55, 57, 58, 112
Acacia albida 58
Ahal (aholim) 114, 115
Aḥu 21, 22
Akkavit 42
Allon 5, 16, 17, 19, 39, 40
Almond 14, 15, 20, 108, 109, 110
Aloe 114, 115
Anemone 81
Apple, Apple tree 12, 81, 108,
    144, 156
Ar'ar 93, 94, 95
Armon 14
Artemisia, Artemisia absinthum 149
Artichoke 41, 42
Asparagus 149
Aspen 135
Avati'aḥ 14, 101
Aviyonah 122, 123

B

Baca 135
Baluta 9
Barley 30, 31, 87, 88, 89, 136, 138

Bay 112
Baẓal 101, 103
Beetroot 14
Benot shua 18
Berosh (brosh) 19, 73, 74
Bokser 129
Boten 15
Box 74
Bramble 41
Briar 34
Broom 19, 57, 116, 117
"Burning Bush" 27, 28
Bulrush 79

C

Calotropis procera 155
Caper 122, 123, 124, 125, 126, 153,
    154
Carob 28, 66, 112, 127, 128, 129, 130,
    131, 132, 133
Casuarina 45
Cedar 20, 43, 44, 47, 74, 78, 79, 80,
    84, 111–114, 143, 148, 153
Chestnut 14
Citron 1, 131

Citrullus colocynthus 155
Colocynth 50, 151, 155
Coloquintida 131
Corn 31, 34, 88, 104, 139, 144
Corylus 14
Cotton 77
Cucumber 101, 104
Cypress 19, 73, 75, 112

D
Dardar 41, 42
Date, Date palm 8, 17, 18, 32, 44, 66,
    67, 96, 107, 108, 136, 137, 138
Dolev 14

E
Ecbalium Elaterium 155
Egoz 20, 67
Elah 5, 6, 39
Erez (arazim) 20, 111, 112, 114
Esev 101, 102
Eshel 7, 8, 9
Etrog 2, 131

F
Fig 1, 2, 8, 32, 36, 47, 61, 66, 68, 76,
    77, 81, 84,85, 106, 107, 108, 136,
    138, 156
Flax 30, 31, 71
Frankincense 52, 87,147

G
Galbanum 52, 53
Garlic 101, 104
Geloska olives 50
Gid, giddim 150, 151
Grapes 19, 61, 67, 85, 98, 99, 100, 105,
    106, 107, 144, 154, 155, 156, 157
Grass 21, 34, 101

H
Hadas, hadassah 18, 19
Ḥaruv (ḥaruvim) 128, 131
Ḥavaẓelet 81

Hazel 14
Ḥaẓir 101, 102
Heath 93
Ḥiryonim 127
Holm oak 134
Hyssop 28, 43, 78, 79, 80, 111, 148

I
Indigo plant 158

J
Johannisbrot 129
Jordan Kippat 52
Juniper 57, 93, 116

K
Kala ilan 158, 159
Kapparis 123, 124
Kedras 112
Kishu 101
Koẓ 41, 42
Kunras 42

L
La'anah 149, 150, 151
Larch 74, 75, 112
Laurel 135
Leek 101, 104
Lentil 88
Levonah 147
Lily 81, 82, 83
Lime 120
Locust 128
Luz 14, 15

M
Maize 120
Mango 120
Mangrove 37, 38
Manna 150, 151
Maple 66
Mayish 66
Melon 14, 101, 104
Mesukkan 134, 135

Mulberry 84, 108, 135
Myrtle 18, 19, 112

N

Naḥal 114
Narcissus 81
Nekhot (nechot) 127, 148
"Nicholas date" 97
Nikalvasin 96
Niẓan (niẓanim) 81

O

Oak 5, 8, 9, 16, 17, 19, 39. 40, 66,
    74, 112, 133
Oil-tree 112
Oleaster 66
Olive 3, 4, 31, 36, 37, 46, 47, 48, 49,
    50, 66, 68, 107, 108, 136, 138, 144
Onion 101, 102, 103, 104
Onycha 52, 123, 153
Orange 120
Oren 20, 127

P

Palm 17, 18, 45, 68, 80, 89, 96, 113,
    114, 115, 120, 134, 143
Panis graecis 129
Peach 144
Peanut 127
Pepper 147
Pereg 151
Petillat ha-midbar 155
Pine 20, 112, 127, 134
Pistacia 5
Plane, Platanus 6, 14, 112
Plum 144
Pomegranate 8, 19, 36, 47, 61, 62, 63,
    67, 81, 106, 107, 109, 115, 136
Poplar 14
Poppy 14

Q

Quercus calliprinosis 40
Quince 156

R

Radish 50
Raisin 50
Reed grass 21, 22, 79, 80
Retama roetam 116
Rimmon 19
Rose 18, 20, 81, 82, 141
Rosh 149, 151, 157
Rotem 19, 57, 116, 117, 118
Rubus sanctus 28
Rye 30

S

St. John's bread 129
Sam 151
Serekah 25
Sesame 50
Shaked 14, 15, 20, 110
Shittah (shittim) 55, 56, 57, 58, 59, 60,
    112
Shoshanah 18, 81, 82, 83
Shum 101
Si'aḥ 10, 11
S'neh 27, 28, 29
Sodom apple 155, 156
Sorek 25, 26
Sparrow grass 149
Spelt 30
Spice 52, 147, 148
Stacte 52
Sugar cane 137
Sward 9
Sycamore 28, 66, 84, 85, 86

T

Tamar 18, 123
Tamarisk 7, 93
Te'ashur 74, 75
Terebinth 5, 8
Thistle 41, 42, 82
Thorn 34, 41, 82, 83, 113
Tirzah 127

V

Vardina 28

Vered 20, 82,

Vine, Vineyard 1, 19, 20, 25, 34, 47, 50, 66, 67, 81, 85, 98, 99, 108, 115, 124, 125, 136, 155, 156

W

Walnut 20, 47, 50, 66, 67, 68, 69, 108, 109, 127

Weed 34, 41, 142

Wheat 1, 30, 87, 88, 136

Willow 36

Wormwood 149, 150, 151

Y

Yerikat ha-ḥamor 155

Z

Zelaf 122, 123

Temple Israel

Minneapolis, Minnesota

DONATED BY
HARRY CARL COWL